PRAEGER WORLD OF ART SERIES

A concise history
of Russian art

1 Map showing some of the principal towns, sites, and religious foundations which are important for the history of the country's art and architecture

A concise history of
RUSSIAN ART

Tamara Talbot Rice

PRAEGER PUBLISHERS
NEW YORK . WASHINGTON

BOOKS THAT MATTER

Published in the United States of America in 1963
by Praeger Publishers, Inc.
111 Fourth Avenue, New York, N.Y. 10003
Fourth printing, 1974
© Thames and Hudson, Ltd. 1963, in London, England
All rights reserved
Library of Congress Catalog Card Number: 63–16653

ISBN 0–275–70150–6

Printed in Great Britain

Contents

In addition to those who so generously made photographs available to me, and whose names will be found under the List of Illustrations, I wish to express my sincere gratitude to Mrs Herbert A. May and Mr George Hann for allowing me to illustrate objects from their collections, to Dr Marvyn Ross, my husband and Mr Jacob Black for their unfailing help, and to Mr Terence Hodgkinson for his assistance.

T.T.R.

Russia Prior to the Mongol Invasion

Although the decorative arts had flourished in various sections of what is today Russian territory from as early as the third millennium B.C., and some tomb constructions of architectural interest had been produced there during the first millennium B.C., it is, nevertheless, customary to associate the beginnings of Russian art with the country's conversion to Christianity in the year 988–89. Indeed, monumental art in the true sense of the term had not existed prior to that date, for it was not until the Russians experienced a need for churches that they discovered within themselves a genius for architecture. If Peter the Great set out to provide Russia with a window facing towards Europe when he founded St Petersburg in the eighteenth century, Vladimir, Grand Duke of Kievan Russia from 978 to 1015, similarily, though unknowingly, opened wide the door which was to lead the Russians to a new world of visual and spiritual creativeness when he adopted Christianity as his own and his people's religion.

The motives which induced Vladimir to become a Christian are today far less important than the consequences which resulted from his decision, yet it is impossible not to wonder whether he was not to some extent inspired by a desire to keep pace with the times rather than because of any very profound religious conviction; or perhaps he was also moved by his desire to marry Anne, sister of the Emperor of Byzantium—a wish which, in its turn, may just as well have been the outcome of a romantic attachment as of any purely political consideration. Vladimir's conversion had no doubt been fostered over the years by Byzantine statesmen in an endeavour to spare the Empire, already weakened by Moslem incursions on its borders and by Iconoclast dissensions at home, from the danger of continued Slavonic attacks. The first of these had occurred as far back as the year 860; Oleg had launched another in 907 when he was able to

7

lead his army to the very walls of Constantinople. Further invasions seemed possible, but a more pressing danger was the threat to the Greek colony of Chersonesus, the northernmost outpost of the Byzantine Empire which many a politician must have wished to maintain as a springboard northward. Such a policy may well have been at the root of the official invitations to Vladimir's grandmother, the Grand Duchess Olga, to visit Constantinople. In 957 she was welcomed there with the utmost pomp, the Byzantine Emperor receiving her seated on the magnificent throne of Solomon, which he used only on the grandest of State occasions. It was then that Olga became converted to the Greek-Orthodox faith. Her baptism took place in Justinian's superb Cathedral of the Holy Wisdom, at a ceremony conducted jointly by the Patriarch of Constantinople and the Emperor of Byzantium. Christianity cannot have come as something entirely new to Olga, for at least three churches already existed in Kiev in her day, but the beauty of the Greek-Orthodox ritual and the magnificence of the setting provided for it at Constantinople must have proved a stirring revelation.

Vladimir's choice of Greek-Orthodoxy in preference to Roman Catholicism may indeed have been in part determined, as the earlier Russian chroniclers imply, by aesthetic considerations, for the Russians have from the earliest times shown themselves quick in the appreciation of beauty. Happening when it did, his choice resulted in the establishment of an almost exclusive link with Byzantium, not only in the religious sphere, but also with regard to cultural and artistic life. Kiev's extensive commercial contacts with Europe, which at times extended as far west as Regensburg, might well have enabled the newly converted Principality to become integrated with Western Europe had not the animosity which separated the Orthodox faith of Constantinople from the Catholic Church of Rome inevitably forced the newly christianized State to become firmly associated with Byzantium. Rome seems tacitly to have recognized the situation, for although a number of divines visited Kiev, and although commercial cities such as Novgorod took every opportunity to expand their western trade, no papal legate was ever appointed to Kiev. Yaroslav (1019–54), Vladimir's younger son and successor, attempted to bring his country into European affairs, but he was never able to weave the Kievan State into the European framework, even though he himself married the Swedish princess Ingigerd, and three of his sons married the daughters of German princes and only the fourth a Byzantine princess, while one of his daughters became the wife of the King of France, another of the King of Hungary, and a third of the King of Norway.

Yet, although the Kievan State was thrown back upon Byzantium, so that its cultural and spiritual life stemmed wholly from Greek sources, it became neither a colony of nor even an area subservient to Byzantium. In spite of the fact that at first the Primate of the Russian Church—a prelate with the rank of metropolitan—was a Greek appointed by the Patriarch of Constantinople; notwithstanding that the creed and all else connected with the country's religion hailed from Byzantium; even though the entire concept of Kievan civilization was acquired from that Empire, still Russia remained independent, and everything adopted from the Greek world began virtually from the start to acquire a life and character of its own. The fact that so much was taken over from Byzantium was not due to Russian indolence, nor to indifference, nor even was it for the sake of expediency; it was an entirely conscious process inspired by a sincere admiration for the Byzantine achievement, which evoked a profound and spontaneous response from the innermost depths of the Russian nature, thereby releasing to the full the spring of Russian creativeness.

That it should have done so is hardly to be wondered at, since, from the earliest times of which we have any knowledge, the inhabitants of the South Russian plain, and especially those in the vicinity of Kiev—the area which has in consequence often been described as the cradle of Russian civilization—had come into contact with various alien cultures and had thereby acquired both the ability to select from these foreign cultures the elements which were most advantageous, and the skill to adapt them to their own need. Thus the Slav artists of both the late pagan and the Early Christian periods had remained unaffected by Scandinavian, or rather Varangian art, in spite of the fact that many of the Kievan princes including Rurik, the founder

9

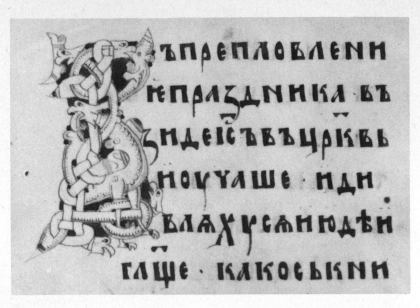

2 A capital letter from a Gospel dated to 1346 in which a bird of Oriental character is intertwined in a Norse interlace, the extremities of which terminate in birds' heads bearing a distinct resemblance to those which appear in Scythian art

of the ruling house, were of Norse extraction, and although a constant stream of Scandinavian merchants travelled along Russia's great waterways, and numerous Varangian mercenaries continued over the years to enlist in the defence forces of the major Russian towns. Only occasionally do Norse elements appear, as for instance in the interlace patterns on the jewellery, especially on bracelets (*Ill. 3*) and buckles, on an infrequent stone capital or, more important, in the decoration of manuscripts (*Ill. 2*). In exactly the same way the Scythians, some thirteen hundred years before, had made wide use in their decorative arts of both Achaemenid and Greek motifs, but had not reacted to the beauty of Persian or Greek architecture.

Indeed, though primitive and uncultured, the tenth-century Kievan was far from being a barbarian, and the objects which he produced were generally of such high quality that they were sure of a ready sale among his more sophisticated neighbours, whether living in Eastern Europe, Byzantium, or Central Asia. Excavations at Tsarskoe Gorodishche, the site of the seventh- and eighth-century city of Rostov, have revealed not only spinning-wheels, planes, axes, potters' implements, and other tools, but also pounded colours and moulds for fashioning articles in silver, bronze, and copper. The objects which were produced by these early Slavs retained many very ancient features in their decoration; especially characteristic are variants of the Great Goddess and the Tree of Life, geometric forms of symbolic content, and of the female figure combined with bird attributes (*Ill. 4*), whether derived from a pigeon, duck or, most often, a swan, though such figures disappeared with the Mongol invasion, as did the naturalistic heads produced during this period by Kievans responding to the influence of Hellenistic art. Other motifs popular at the time show the influence of Scythian and Goth designs, and the Slavs also probably derived from them such Oriental motifs as the griffin or the sirin, the female bird whose songs, according to Russian legends, beguile the saints in Paradise (*Ill. 86*). Many a design with which the peasant women continued until the Revolution to adorn their ritual towels and bed curtains, working them either in red cross-stitch embroidery or in drawn thread work, must also have survived from Scythian times. Horse forms on the other hand were

3 This silver bangle was found on the site of Kiev's Mikhailov-Zlatoverkh Monastery. It dates from the twelfth century and its decorations include birds of Byzantine origin, heraldic-looking beasts of Oriental character, and interlace designs of Scandinavian inspiration

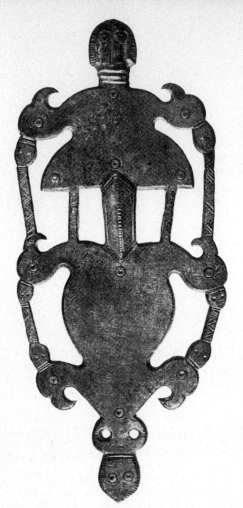

4 A cast bronze clasp of seventh-century date from the village of Zenkova in the Poltava district. The habit of associating bird attributes with a female figure was sufficiently widespread in early medieval times to suggest that designs of this type were invested with some sort of magical or ritualistic significance

introduced into folk art by the pagan Slavs who evolved them when, as sun-worshippers, they used pictorial renderings of the horse to symbolize the steeds who drew Apollo on his daily course across the hemisphere. The moulded silver gilt figure of a horse (*Ill. 5*) of sixth-century date from Martynovka, near Kiev, still retains many features proper to Scythian art, though it is more stylized.

The eleventh and twelfth centuries were periods of immense intellectual activity throughout the civilized world, whether Islamic or Christian. In the Middle East the Seljuks were creating a civilization, the quality of which, though it is only now coming to be appreciated

5 A cast silver amulet in the form of a horse dating from the sixth century. Found at Martynovka near Kiev with others which included human figures. They all bear a clear resemblance to objects produced between the fifth and third centuries B.C. by Scythian and kindred nomads of the Eurasian steppe

at its true worth, greatly influenced contemporary intellectuals; in Western Europe the reawakening of the creative spirit was responsible for the growth of Romanesque art; in Sicily and Venice it inspired a series of superb mosaic decorations; in ancient Christian kingdoms such as Georgia and Armenia native cultures of proven vigour were producing works of art of the first importance, though they continue to be but little known in the Western world. Yet Constantinople remained the primary centre of art and culture; nowhere else were ideas more dynamic and diversified, nowhere was anything more sophisticated or superb to be found. It is thus not surprising that it was by Byzantium that Russia was most inspired. In Constantinople the blend of ancient and modern, of robust entertainments and pietistic Scholasticism, of immense luxury and fervent asceticism had been revivified in the ninth century by a wave of enthusiasm evoked by the downfall of the Iconoclasts.

The delight which Greek intellectuals took in Hellenistic art was, however, shared only by the small number of Russians who visited Byzantium. Vladimir was among the few who responded to the fascination of the antique, bringing back to Kiev from Chersonesus not only Christianity with all that the new creed required, but also two Classical statues and four bronze horses which probably resembled those which still adorn St Mark's at Venice, but which then stood in Constantinople. But none of these sculptures appear to have made any impression on the Kievans, where no artist thought of working in the Classical vein, and only Mstislav, Prince of Chernigov and Tmutorokan, when building in 1036 the Cathedral of the Transfiguration in his capital of Chernigov, used marble columns of ancient origin to support its dome instead of the piers that were becoming customary. The result, whether or not due to expediency, cannot have proved popular, for although it was the Cathedral of Chernigov which influenced the exterior of Novgorod's Hagia Sophia, and thereby Russian architecture as a whole, yet practically all the architects who were inspired by it used piers instead of columns in their churches. The substitution cannot be wholly ascribed to economic considerations for although the greater cost of marble columns would have limited their use it would not have entirely excluded it.

Christianity brought many changes to Russia. By insisting upon monogamy it struck at every household including Vladimir's own, for the Grand Duke is credited with having had some three hundred concubines at the time of his conversion. By forbidding human sacrifices and blood feuds it raised the dignity and value of human life. By the adoption of the Slavonic alphabet, originally devised for use in Bulgaria by the saintly scholars Cyril and Methodius, it created a new class of educated men. Indeed, the Church's battle against ignorance and illiteracy introduced a new conception of law, it opened the road to the study of medicine and allied subjects such as botany and zoology, as well as that of humanistic learning and intellectual pastimes. But the greatest and most obvious change was the one created visually by the architects and artists who were imported from Byzantium, for it fell to them to carry out the first phase of the transformation which was soon to alter the Russian scene completely.

At his conversion Vladimir gave orders for all things connected with pagan worship to be destroyed and the primitive temples and totem-pole-like idols were swept away from the market squares. In their place churches had to be established. The Russians had been handling wood, which was the local building material, for centuries, and many of the minor churches which were hurriedly put up at the time were wooden structures. But Vladimir was determined that the cathedral churches should be in masonry so as to prove worthy of the new faith and that they might at the same time endow Kiev with something of Constantinople's beauty. It was this decision which made it necessary for him to turn to Byzantium, or sometimes perhaps also to the neighbouring Greek city of Chersonesus, not only for his priests and church furnishings, but also for his architects and artists.

The Greeks who responded to Vladimir's call brought to Kievan Russia the fully developed styles of tenth-century Byzantium, but since many of them came from the Empire's provincial centres it was not always the most up-to-date or fashionable trends of eleventh-century Constantinople that were adopted. Vladimir's only important foundation—that of the Church of the Assumption—was largely a Greek building, but although constructed of brick and stone by a Greek architect, its foundations were made of oak in what was at the time the traditional Russian manner. Begun in 989 and completed within three years, it was a cruciform building with three apses and a roof resting on piers. Vladimir set aside a tenth of his revenue for its upkeep, so that it came later to be known as the Church of the Dime. In 1240 the Mongols who besieged Kiev directed their catapults at its dome, and when they eventually broke into the town they completed its destruction. The church of the same name which stood on the original site until its removal in 1939 dated only from the nineteenth century; it was the work of the eminent architect Stassov. Recent excavations have shown that the original building had been decorated with floor and wall mosaics and that in 1039 the number of its aisles had been increased from three to five.

15

Fortunately, two of Russia's greatest cathedrals were built within fifty years of Vladimir's Church of the Dime. Both survive to our day, even though the one underwent considerable if superficial alterations at the hands of eighteenth-century Baroque architects, whilst the other suffered grievously in the course of the last war. Both were foundations of Vladimir's successor, Yaroslav. Following Constantinople's example, both were dedicated to Hagia Sophia or the Holy Wisdom, that is to say to the Saviour, and both were built as cathedral churches. One was situated in Kiev, the other in Novgorod, but Kiev being the capital, it was Kiev's Hagia Sophia which was invested with the greater symbolic meaning. Its esoteric significance was partly due to its role of prime cathedral and coronation church, and partly to the fact that the site chosen was one on which Yaroslav had inflicted a crippling defeat on the Pecheneg nomads, thereby ensuring Kiev's security. It was surely not by chance that the centre of the cathedral's main apse fell on the point at which two lines drawn from each of the city's four gates intersected. The Grand Duke himself laid the cathedral's foundation-stone in 1036–37; the building was of brick, set in a pinkish cement, and the architect and master mason came from Byzantium, but Lazarev has shown that Russian labourers were employed on the work as well as Greek ones. Yaroslav and his Russian Metropolitan, Hilarion, took a deep interest in the work and were, in the opinion of Lazarev, responsible for many of the cathedral's features. It may well have been that Yaroslav employed all the Russians capable of building in brick at Kiev in much the same way that Peter the Great in the eighteenth century concentrated all available stone and brick in St Petersburg. If this was so, it would serve to explain why Novgorod's first Hagia Sophia was built of wood; but the fact that the contemporary cathedral at Chernigov was of masonry suggests rather that the use of wood at Novgorod was more probably due to a local fondness for a material in the handling of which the region's craftsmen had long excelled.

Both the Russian Hagia Sophias closely followed a Byzantine plan, each being cruciform with several aisles and domes, but Kiev's was by far the more elaborate (*Ill. 6*). It contained five aisles and was

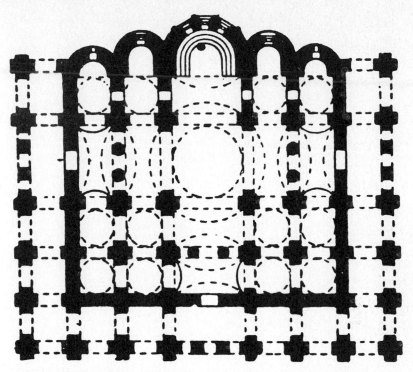

6 Plan after Alpatov of the Cathedral of Hagia Sophia, Kiev, 1036–46

greater in width than in length, but a feature which seldom occurred elsewhere was the introduction of a single-storeyed peristyle running round its north, south, and west walls and opening into the town's main square, with porphyry, marble, and alabaster columns supporting the arches of the west front. Russian taste already at this early date managed to express itself clearly in a large central dome symbolizing Christ, rising from amidst twelve smaller ones representing the Apostles. The Byzantines had never indulged in such a galaxy of domes, though their drums were more ornate than the Russian ones and were pierced with larger windows. Novgorod's wooden Hagia Sophia was likewise roofed with thirteen domes; indeed the dome became both an architectural necessity and the expression of a spiritual aspiration of Russia, riveting attention on

17

7 The west front of the Cathedral of Hagia Sophia, Kiev, as it is today, showing the additions made in the Baroque style during an eighteenth-century restoration

the celestial sphere which the Scriptures portrayed as existing, if almost unattainable, but which the architects invested with a convincing reality. Aesthetically, it transformed the Russian skyline, giving it an elevation which nature had failed to provide in that universally flat countryside. In small churches, where there was only one dome, it was placed near the east end of the roof; in more elaborate ones, where there were three, they were grouped close together and kept to the same size; in the case of five-domed churches the central one was given greater height than the others.

Kiev's Hagia Sophia (*Ill. 7*) appears to rise like some great natural growth, resembling in this Hagia Sophia at Constantinople, but whereas the latter emphasizes its oneness with its site by reserving its adornments for its interior, Kiev's bore the imprint of man's artistry on its façade no less than within its walls. Nevertheless, the Kievan Hagia Sophia's accord with its setting is the earliest example of the irresistible effect which the Russian environment and Russian taste exercised over the foreign architects and artists who found employment there throughout the centuries. Regardless of their origins, even

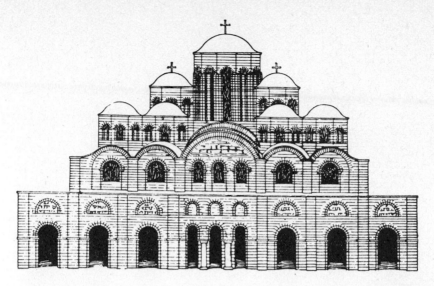

8 Reconstruction after Alpatov of the west front of the Cathedral of Hagia Sophia, Kiev, as it appeared in the eleventh century

the fully formed artists produced from the start works which were so strongly imbued with the Russian spirit that they differ completely from everything that these artists had created in their native lands before going to Russia. This is as true of Kiev's Hagia Sophia as of Moscow's Kremlin or Leningrad's Winter Palace, for even though the first's massive, horizontal shape was never to become as typical of Russia as Chernigov Cathedral's more perpendicular lines, Kiev's Hagia Sophia is nevertheless quite distinct from anything that was built at the time in Byzantium, and it contains moreover many of the essentials from which the medieval style of Russian church architecture developed.

When restored to its original form, that is to say when visualized stripped of its Baroque additions, Kiev's Hagia Sophia is remarkable for its monolithic yet superbly elegant appearance. Much of this distinction is due to the inclusion, above the rounded arches of the peristyle, of a row of shallow, well-proportioned, oval alcoves (*Ill. 8*). Equally unusual for its date is the row of windows set above the niches; the transition from the rounded arches to the oval niches, and

9 Detail showing the mosaic head of St Basil the Great from the full-length figures of saints adorning the south side of the main apse of the Cathedral of Hagia Sophia, Kiev, dating from the mid eleventh century

thence to the rectangular windows is accomplished with consummate mastery; any suggestion of monotony is cleverly avoided, and the skill shown in the spacing and treatment of the windows is dictated by an essentially Russian talent, one which is also well to the fore in medieval Novgorodian building, but which is perhaps to be seen at its most successful in Petersburgian architecture.

In its interior, with its multiplicity of marble columns and arches, of vistas and galleries, Kiev's Hagia Sophia presents a typically Byzantine complexity and sophistication, unique in Russia, excelling in the variety of its effects those achieved in such a building as St Mark's at Venice. Indeed, nothing quite so grand and vibrant existed anywhere else in Western Europe at the time. At Kiev the feeling of vitality within the cathedral, or rather of actuality, was, as Lazarev points out, sustained by the mosaics. The effect was due partly to the scintillations produced by the light catching the gold and delicately coloured cubes, but still more to the frontal pose of the figures (*Ill. 9*), which invests the personages with the character of an audience, suggesting that they are both participating in and

10 This superb mosaic of St Demetrius dates from the latter half
of the eleventh century and is made of glass, stone, and marble cubes.
It is one of the few fragments to survive from the important series
of mosaics which adorned the church of the Mikhailov-Zlatoverkh
Monastery at Kiev

also watching all that takes place within the church. Lazarev dates the first of the mosaics—those in the main dome and its drum—to 1046, the year in which the cathedral's structure was completed, and the others to no later than 1067; they thus fall between those of Hosios Lucas in Greece (early eleventh century) on the one hand and those of Vatopedi on Mount Athos on the other. The traditional scenes appear in their prescribed positions on the walls; Lazarev ascribes them to Greek designers of provincial origin because their style is closer to tenth-century Byzantine works than to the Constantinopolitan manner of their own day. He sees the master's hand in the row of saints on the north side of the apse, but he also draws attention to certain peculiarities, such as features of Russian cast among the other saints, which he ascribes to the participation of Russian mosaicists, making a good case for regarding these important decorations as Russo-Byzantine works in the same way that the mosaics of Sicily are described by Demus as Graeco-Sicilian ones. Graffiti found on the walls include Russian inscriptions as well as Slavonic and Greek ones, and so seem to confirm this view, as does the discovery in Kiev during recent excavations of the sites of three distinct workshops in which glass mosaic cubes were made. At Hagia Sophia, Lazarev found that no less than a hundred and seventeen different shades of cubes were used to produce the desired effects.

References survive to three other great Kievan churches containing mosaic decorations which pre-dated the Mongol invasion, and their number was probably greater than this. Nothing now survives of the mosaics which adorned the church which Svyatoslav built between 1073 and 1078 in the Monastery of the Caves and dedicated to the Assumption, nor of those which stood in the cathedral church of the Vydubetsk Monastery, but fragments survive of the ones in the Mikhailov-Zlatoverkh Monastery (*Ill. 10*), which is often referred to as the Dmitrov. Lazarev again attributes them to the Graeco-Russian school; they date from the end of the eleventh or the early twelfth century, yet differ markedly in style from those of Hagia Sophia, in some instances recalling certain far earlier panels to be seen in the Cathedral of St Demetrius at Salonica; but the majority already reveal a fondness for the peculiarly Russian shade of pink

11 These painted portraits of four of the Grand Duke Yaroslav's five daughters in Hagia Sophia, Kiev, must, according to Professor Lazarev, be dated to about 1045 for the eldest daughter, Elizabeth, was married to the future King of Norway in 1044-45, when she was about twenty years old; at that time the second daughter, who was later to become Queen of France, would have been about seventeen

which frequently recurs in Muscovite enamels. In general, however, mosaics proved too expensive and required too large a number of highly skilled technicians for them to have become widely used, and, instead, wall-paintings assumed at an early date a position of immense importance in Russian church decoration.

Wall-paintings had from the start played a prominent part in Kiev's Hagia Sophia. In addition to biblical scenes of customary Byzantine character, a panel running along the outer face of the north, south, and east gallery walls (*Ill. 11*) showed, at the centre of the east face, the figure of the Saviour receiving from Yaroslav a model of the cathedral; behind Yaroslav his sons were ranged in order of seniority and opposite to him his wife and daughters, all in single file. All the central figures, that is to say those of the Saviour,

12 A fresco of two actors, one masked, fighting. From the eleventh-century series of paintings on the stairs of the north tower of Hagia Sophia, Kiev, showing scenes from the Games held at the Hippodrome in Constantinople

Yaroslav and his wife, three of their sons, and their eldest daughter have disappeared, but the portraits of four daughters survive on the south wall and of two sons on the north. They are shown in attitudes of adoration, the elder children holding long tapers. All wear the Court dress of the day; their robes are made of foreign brocades cut on simpler lines than the Byzantine models which they resemble. Each portrait reflects more of the children's individualities than might have been expected at this period.

Quite distinct and unique in their choice of subjects are the paintings which decorate the walls of the fine staircase which linked the adjacent palace to the cathedral and leads to the Grand Duke's private pew, situated, as in Constantinople's Hagia Sophia, in the centre of the west gallery. In contrast to any surviving Byzantine paintings the subjects chosen for these decorations illustrate secular instead of biblical themes (*Ill. 12, 13*); they depict the mimes, jugglers, musicians, wrestlers, dancers, and animal tamers who took part in the so-called Goth Games held, according to Constantine Porphyro-

13 Another of the eleventh-century secular paintings from the north tower of the Cathedral of Hagia Sophia, Kiev, this time showing a musician playing a string instrument

genitus, in the Hippodrome at Constantinople on the ninth day of Christmas in the presence of the factions, each member of which wore his team's colours. Russian notables visiting Constantinople greatly enjoyed the Games organized in their honour; the delight which Yaroslav derived from such pastimes as well as from hunting can be inferred from the numerous criticisms which they evoked from Russian churchmen of his day, but the Grand Duke must have disregarded their strictures, since he had the walls of his private staircase within the cathedral's precincts decorated with the scenes which amused him.

Many of the craftsmen who helped to create the great pictorial and architectural masterpieces of Early Christian Russian art were Russians. Those responsible for the fine book illuminations, delicate cloisonné enamels, and superbly chased or embossed pieces of jewellery and metalwork of both secular and religious character have remained anonymous, and so too have the majority of the builders and painters, but the early chronicles praise among others

25

the carpenter Mironeg, who lived in the first half of the eleventh century, and the builder Jdan Nikola, who worked throughout its closing decades. Most admired of all, however, was the painter Alimpi, a monk of the Monastery of the Caves at Kiev, who died there in 1114. The fine icon of the Virgin of Svensk (*Ill. 14*), now in the Tretyakov Gallery in Moscow, was for a time thought to be by his hand; although it is now assigned to the end of the thirteenth century, its iconography is peculiar to Alimpi's monastery so that it is more than likely that this noble painting closely resembles Alimpi's icon—it may well indeed have been copied from it.

So many churches were built in Kiev that less than fifty years after the country's conversion Thietmar of Merseburg, who visited the capital in 1018, asserted that their number ran to almost four hundred. Kiev was not alone in its zeal; most other towns displayed a similar fervour, attempting in their larger cathedrals, as in the case of the second Hagia Sophia of Novgorod, built in stone, and the individualistic cathedral of the same name built at Polotsk, to contend with Kiev's splendour. It was an age of experiment and test; the national style was in the making, and although Novgorod was to fashion it and create its golden age, a group of quite distinct, supremely lovely and graceful churches were built by four rulers of the Vladimir-Suzdalian Principality between the years 1150 and 1250 or so. Perhaps acting to some extent at the instigation of Vladimir Monomachus, Grand Duke of Kiev, the style was introduced by Yuri Dolgoruki (died 1157) in a virtually fully fledged form. Many of its basic elements, such as a square or rectangular ground plan containing a three-aisled cruciform church and a domed roof came from Kiev, but an elevation based on the cube and the elongation of the dome's drum created a new effect which was maintained by an entirely unprecedented use of external sculptured decoration.

Much of the district of Vladimir-Suzdal consisted of forests so that its inhabitants were accustomed to build in wood, yet the churches founded by Yuri Dolgoruki as well as his son and successor Andrei Bogolyubski (died 1174), and by the latter's heir and follower on the throne, Vsevolod III (1176–1212) are built in white Kama sandstone. They were not, however, given solid walls; they were made

14 Icon of the Virgin of Svensk, a thirteenth-century work for a time attributed to Alimpi. It follows a type peculiar to the monastery so may well be a copy of the first Russian painting mentioned by early chroniclers. Antonij and Feodorij, the founders of the monastery, appear on either side of the Virgin

15 The Church of the Saviour at Pereyaslavl-Zalessk dates from 1152 and is one of the earliest examples of Vladimir-Suzdalian architecture to have survived. Its restrained decoration foreshadows the use to which sculpture was soon to be put

of two parallel stone partitions with the intervening space filled in with rubble over which cement was poured to form a setting. The method was perhaps the result of inexperience, but it probably contributed to the elegant appearance of the churches, which are the lightest and most graceful to be found in Russia. The earliest in the group, the churches at Kidersha and at Pereyaslavl-Zalessk (*Ill. 15*), were both built by Yuri Dolgoruki in 1152; like the later examples, their three aisles terminate in apses at the east end and four central piers support the single dome of their roofs. Each church contained a gallery and in each case the external elevation

16 The south front of the Cathedral of St Dmitri at Vladimir, 1194–97, showing the extent to which sculptured decoration was being used in Vladimir within some forty years of the appearance of the style. Whilst Oriental influences are to the fore in the decorations of the upper section, Western ones predominate below

was cube-shaped, a narrow, cylindrical drum upholding the dome. Andrei Bogolyubski brought the style to its full beauty. It is to be seen in its purity in the church which he built in 1165 on the banks of the River Nerl to commemorate the death of his favourite son, Izyaslav. Dedicated to the Virgin, it is a building which is singularly

17 Plan after Alpatov of the Cathedral of St George at Yuriev-Polski

well attuned to its enchanting setting; it is also among the first to display on its outer walls high relief figural sculptures of the type which were to prove characteristic of the group, and its cylindrical drum is adorned with no less typical sculptures of a geometric type, though these may have originated in the Novgorodian area rather than in Vladimir-Suzdal. The severe window and door surrounds are undoubtedly a local feature, though more ornate ones were later to appear at Pskov, and, later still, architects working under Italian influence in Moscow and Yaroslavl were to frame their windows and doors with lace-like sculptures or glazed tile work.

The figural, animal, or floral sculptures which appear on the later churches of this group of Vladimir-Suzdalian churches almost cover the outer walls of the buildings. Especially characteristic are those decorating the Cathedral of St Dmitri (*Ill. 16*) at Vladimir (1194–97) and that of St George (*Ill. 17, 18*) at Yuriev-Polski (1230–34). The sculptures on both are so curious in style that it is difficult to account for them, some seeming to reflect the influence of Western Europe, others of the East, and more especially of Georgia. Indeed, each of these elements could equally well have made itself felt in twelfth-century Vladimir, for groups of Romanesque craftsmen are

18 The Cathedral of St George at Yuriev-Polski, 1230–34, is the last important church built in the Vladimir-Suzdalian style. Its outer walls are covered in a mass of sculptured decorations executed by different hands in various styles

known to have travelled considerable distances in search of work, and may well have penetrated as far eastward, whilst contacts with the Caucasus were so close that they resulted in Andrei Bogolyubski's youngest son, though Prince of Novgorod in 1174, eventually becoming the first husband of the famous Georgian queen Tamara. Contemporary documents provide no solution, for although the chronicles state that 'Andrei sought no craftsmen among the Germans' (the word German being used in Russia almost into modern times to describe all Westerners), they also mention that 'God brought artists to Andrei from all parts of the earth.'

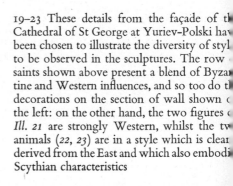

20

19–23 These details from the façade of the Cathedral of St George at Yuriev-Polski have been chosen to illustrate the diversity of style to be observed in the sculptures. The row of saints shown above present a blend of Byzantine and Western influences, and so too do the decorations on the section of wall shown on the left: on the other hand, the two figures of *Ill. 21* are strongly Western, whilst the two animals (*22, 23*) are in a style which is clearly derived from the East and which also embodies Scythian characteristics

21

23

On both the Cathedral of St Dmitri at Vladimir and St George
at Yuriev-Polski the sculptures cover the north, south, and west
walls of the buildings (*Ill. 19–23*). The majority are executed in low
relief and are to some extent reminiscent of wood-carving. A few
savour of the West; many more reflect Eastern influence, both in the
proportions of the figures and the choice of motifs; others—such as
the surface design forming the background on the slabs of the east
wall of the Cathedral of St George—are reminiscent of Georgian
metalwork; one or two details suggest links with the Seljuks, whose
influence had already made itself felt in the masonry of some churches
built round about the year 1200 in the neighbourhood of Chersonesus;

24 The Scythian elements which appear in the Vladimir-Suzdalian sculptures shown on *Ill.* 22 and 23 are integral elements of Russian folk art, persisting in the needlework, and painted and carved work produced by peasants of our time. They are easily discernible in this piece of drawn thread work produced in Nizhni-Novgorod (Gorki) early in the nineteenth century

most interesting of all are the fairly numerous motifs which retain Scythian elements; these are especially evident in the winged lions, griffin-headed birds, and other fantastic animals of a type which remained popular in peasant embroidery in modern times and which, in Vladimir-Suzdal, still retains traces of the Scythian dot and comma muscle markings (*Ill. 24*). In contrast, some of the floral sculptures, notably those in the lower sections of the blind arcades decorating the south and north walls of the Cathedral of St Dmitri, though leaving no immediate followers, foreshadow the bronze decorations on the deep blue or opaque white enamels produced for Catherine the Great; however, a similar strip on the south wall displays Scandinavian influence in its interlace designs, whilst that used to offset the Byzantinesque saints on the north wall shows stronger affinities with the West.

The Russian element in the country's Byzantinesque churches pre-dating the Mongol invasion are clearly to be seen when any one of these buildings is compared with a Byzantine one of a like date. The same phenomenon occurs also in early Russian painting, though, to begin with, it does so to a lesser degree. The first manuscripts and icons used in Russia were Greek works brought for the most part from Chersonesus rather than the Byzantine mainland, but they were soon followed by outstanding examples of Constantinopolitan work-manship. The icons which were first produced on Russian soil were probably also the works of Greeks, doubtless of the same artists as those employed on the mural decorations of the churches, but although the interiors of at any rate all the more important churches formed veritable picture galleries devoted to themes derived from

25 An illumination from the Svyatoslav Codex, 1073, showing a Council of Bishops assembled within a richly decorated church

the Scriptures, the Russians seem to have shown from the start a greater fondness for icons than for mural paintings. This may in part have resulted from psychological causes, for the Russians appear to have sought in their new religion the humanistic elements which were wholly absent from the harsh and cruel creeds of their pagan days. Even the earliest of the mural and manuscript decorations (*Ill. 25*) carried out in Russia by Greek or native artists already diffuse a stronger sense of gentleness and understanding than is to be found in contemporary Byzantine work; nevertheless, the air of remoteness which envelopes the personages depicted on the walls, and which is due as much to their elevated positions on them as to the frontal manner in which they are presented, and to the convention whereby all holy personages and even saints were larger in size than ordinary people, tended to stress the difference separating the worshippers from the celestial sphere to which they aspired. The distance dividing the people from their icons was less marked, partly because of the smaller size of even the largest panels, partly too because, until the introduction of the iconostasis, the position of even the highest placed icons was only slightly above eye-level.

The Byzantine icon which is known to us today as the *Virgin of Vladimir* (*Ill. 26*) is a masterpiece of outstanding quality. Its beauty and importance was fully realized by the Kievans, and both the Lavrentiev and the Ipatiev chronicles devote considerable attention to it. They inform us that when Mstislav, a son of Vladimir Monomachus, decided to build a church in the Pirogoshcha district of Kiev, to be dedicated to the Virgin, he commissioned an icon of the Virgin and Child in Byzantium for it. The Prince laid the foundation-stone of his church in 1132, the building being completed within four years; by that time the icon he had ordered for it had reached Kiev, together with a second painting of the Virgin and Child, which it seems reasonable to suppose had been commissioned from the same artist. The icon destined for the church has disappeared long ago, and not even a description of it survives; fate dealt more kindly with the second panel which is the one which is known to us today as the *Virgin of Vladimir* because it was transported in 1167 to Vladimir, the city which superseded Kiev as capital of Russia. The icon became so closely associated with its new home that even after its removal to Moscow late in the fourteenth century the connexion was perpetuated in the name by which the painting continued to be known.

The icon of the *Virgin of Vladimir* shows a degree of tenderness which is quite unusual for its date, the Virgin's head touching the Child's in a gesture of such deep affection that, iconographically, the rendering bears the designation of 'tenderness'. Though the work of

26 Icon of the *Virgin of Vladimir;* early twelfth century. This Byzantine painting was specially commissioned for Kiev in Byzantium, but shortly after its arrival in Kiev it was moved to Vladimir, whence it took its name. In 1395 it was set up in the Cathedral of the Assumption in the Kremlin at Moscow and came to be regarded as the pallium of Russia

27 The Vernicle—painting on the face of a late-twelfth-century panel which stood, until the Revolution, in the Cathedral of the Assumption at Moscow, and was one of the first to undergo cleaning and preservation, the work being undertaken in 1919 by the USSR State Restoration Workshops

what must assuredly have been one of Constantinople's greatest painters, the spirit which it manifests is so profoundly Russian that it must have been introduced into the icon at the specific wish of the Prince who commissioned the panel. In Russia the painting inspired an iconographic prototype which thereafter remained among the most deeply loved; it set a standard for monumental representations of the Virgin and Child which all subsequent artists strove to attain;

28 The reverse of the icon of the Vernicle illustrated on the preceding plate shows the Adoration of the Cross, a contemporary work by a different hand. Though at this date all religious paintings were produced by servants of the church, this painting bears the imprint of a monk's rather than a priest's hand

in addition it seems to have been one of the earliest examples of the gentler, more humanistic type of religious art which developed in Russia through the years within the Byzantine framework.

It is not customary to ascribe to Kiev any of the surviving Russian icons that date from before the Mongol occupations—some twenty panels at the very most, yet the twelfth-century Annunciation (*Ill. 29*), which was formerly at Ustyug and is now in the Tretyakov

29 This icon is known as the *Ustyug Annunciation* because, although it stood for many centuries in the Cathedral of the Annunciation at Moscow, and although scholars tend to associate it with the Yuriev Monastery at Novgorod, legend firmly connects it with the town of Ustyug. It is an early-twelfth-century work

Gallery in Moscow, has much to suggest that it came from Russia's first capital. The iconography is not the customary Byzantine form in which an angel advances towards the seated Virgin; it is more symbolic, noble, and monumental—it might well be termed Classical, that is to say Hellenistic. The style of the figure suggests familiarity with a long line of ancient masterpieces which only Kiev could have enjoyed. Lazarev is inclined to assign it to a royal workshop. The angel's neatly arranged hair with gold outlines stressing its rhythmical, decorative coils, as well as the oscillations of its wings, are basic features which are to be seen repeated at their best in the twelfth-century icon of the Archangel Gabriel, known as the *Golden-haired Angel* (*Ill. 30*). Though the latter is also generally ascribed to Novgorod, this too seems to bear the imprint of Kiev. The same mannerisms are to be seen again in the oldest known Russian rendering of the Vernicle (*Ill. 27*), though here the style is clearly different. The painting appears on the face of a large processional icon of twelfth-century date. In this instance the innate Russian delight in decorative effects—a delight which is at the basis of the treatment of

30 Icon of the Archangel Gabriel, often called that of the *Golden-haired Angel*; late twelfth century. Lazarev is tempted to ascribe this delicate yet forceful rendering to a royal workshop

the angels on the two icons discussed above—is controlled by an equally Russian feeling for rhythm. It is this feeling which has enabled Russian painters of all periods to appear at their best in the graphic arts. The Saviour's face as shown on this rendering of the Vernicle may also be regarded as a study in curves, as a concept verging on abstraction, yet for all its concern for recurrent lines, the depth of feeling embodied in the painting and the absence from it of any trace of sentimentality raises it to the rank of a masterpiece. The obverse of the icon displays the Adoration of the Cross (*Ill. 28*) and is the work of a different, though contemporary hand. For all its balance it is less lyrical, less inspired, and the amount of symbolic detail introduced into the scene suggests a monk's hand; the Classical touches which can be detected in the figures of the angels provide a link with the *Ustyug Annunciation*, and because of this it is tempting to assign the icon to a large monastic workshop, such as that of the Monastery of the Caves at Kiev.

The small number of early icons of Vladimir-Suzdalian workmanship that survive are to be numbered with Russia's greatest

31 Icon of the Virgin Orans; late twelfth
to early thirteenth century. It was found
in the Spass-Preobrazhensk Monastery and
is generally accepted as a painting of the
school of Yaroslavl. The work of cleaning
and preserving it lasted from 1925 to 1929

pictorial treasures. Among the finest is a large panel of late-twelfth-
or early-thirteenth-century date bearing the Virgin Orans (*Ill. 31*);
it comes from the Monastery of the Saviour at Yaroslavl, and is now
in the Tretyakov Gallery at Moscow. The Virgin, as the iconographic definition implies, is shown standing with raised arms,
bearing on her breast a medallion of Christ Emmanuel with His
arms extended in a similar way. Everything about this painting is of
the highest quality; in it the spacing of the figures, the nobility of
their expression, and the delicacy of the brushwork is matched by the
sensitive, well-balanced, luminous, and expressive colours. Even the
angels' heads within the medallions are major works of art, capable
of enlargement to many times their actual size. The Virgin's immensely tall figure is truly monumental, yet its formality is transfused
by the deep humanism of her expression, the beauty of which is not

32 Icon of St Demetrius of Salonica. The Saint's figure dates to the twelfth century, the details in the background to the fourteenth, sixteenth, and eighteenth centuries. The panel stood for many years in the Church of St Demetrius of Salonica—ever a popular saint in Russia—at Dmitrov, in the district of Moscow and was cleaned in 1923–24. Note the sword held by the Saint, for it was an emblem of royalty in medieval Russia and may indicate that the icon was painted for a royal patron

disturbed by her eyes, which are heavy with unshed tears, nor by her mouth, which is tightly compressed in pain. In contrast, the Child's face, for all its prescience, is irradiated with serenity. Furthermore, the artist was not so entirely engrossed in producing these poignant effects as to forget the importance of decorative detail. Placing his figures on a rug, the design of which is so close to those that appear on some twelfth- and thirteenth-century Konya carpets that it is tempting to assign it to the Seljuks of Anatolia, he turned his attention to the drapery of the Virgin's robes. By handling the folds of her skirt schematically and those of her cloak rhythmically he achieved a forcefulness and variety of effects that are seldom to be met with in paintings of a similar date and character.

The same sense of the monumental and a similar feeling for the decorative is to be seen in the twelfth-century Suzdalian icon of

43

33 Detail showing the right-hand angel from a twelfth-century icon of the Deesis with the Christ Emmanuel of Vladimir-Suzdalian workmanship. It is similar both in shape and style to the more conventional rendering of the Deesis by an artist of the same school shown on *Ill. 34*. Though the latter is several decades later in date both icons are masterpieces of the highest order

St Demetrius of Salonica (*Ill. 32*), where there is also to be noted so marked a Patrician touch that it is difficult not to associate the icon with some member of the reigning house. Even though there is no mention of a Court workshop in any surviving document, the three princes who formed the architectural style of Vladimir-Suzdal may well have had one. St Demetrius is shown on this icon seated on a throne, holding the type of sword which, in medieval Russia, served as the symbol of sovereignty. As in the Virgin Orans the throne stands on a contemporary carpet of Anatolian or Caucasian origin. The Saint's face is as much that of a man following a religious vocation as of an alert military commander, and is a vivid personification of the gallant heroes who figure in Russian folk-lore.

The Patrician element is equally marked in two Deesis panels of the same school. The Deesis theme was extremely popular throughout the Vladimir-Suzdalian Principality, where it epitomized the

intercessionary role which Russians associated with their icons. Lazarev draws attention to an entry under the year 1175 in the Ipatiev chronicle which records that Andrei Bogolyubski never travelled without taking a three-panelled Deesis icon with him. Each of the icons under discussion is painted on a single, long, narrow panel showing only the heads and shoulders of the figures. The earlier icon (*Ill. 33*) is both the more unusual and perhaps the lovelier of the two. Dating from the end of the twelfth century, it presents the young Christ Emmanuel and not, as was usual, the grown man, showing Him between two archangels instead of the more customary figures of the Virgin and St John. The Saviour has all the appearance of a hero-prince of folk-lore, but the archangels, with hair coiled in the Kievan manner, express severity and compassion. The second, more traditional version (*Ill. 34*) is a few decades later in date, belonging to the beginning of the thirteenth rather than the end of the twelfth century. The elegance and dignity which characterize all Suzdalian works of pre-Mongol invasion date, permeating also the very small number of manuscript illuminations which survive, is clearly present in this panel, though something of the virility and originality of the three earlier paintings is lacking. It is perhaps closer in style, though not in spirit, to the fragmentary wall-paintings which survive on the west and south walls of the Cathedral of St Dmitri at Vladimir and to the less well-preserved and rather later ones in the town's Cathedral of the Assumption. The Last Judgement

45

35 The frescoes of the Last Judgement in the Cathedral of the Assumption at Vladimir date from the end of the twelfth century. The cycle of seated apostles, with angels behind them, is largely the work of a Byzantine artist, but the faces are so expressive that his assistants were evidently Russians

is the least damaged and the more important of the cycles which once adorned the walls of the latter cathedral. Only parts survive; they include two groups of Apostles (*Ill. 35*), some holy personages about to enter Paradise, and the figures of Jacob, Isaac, and Abraham seated beneath the trees of Paradise (*Ill. 36*); they represent the souls of the good. Even these few fragments suffice to show the high quality of the work, but they are especially interesting on account of their emotional content for they make no effort to conceal the anxiety and stresses to which those striving to enter Paradise are subjected. They thus present a clear contrast to the figures on the walls of Hagia Sophia at Kiev, where each stands aloof and assured, unaffected by earthly worries of the sort which trouble the Suzdalian Saint. The self-control attained by the Patrician-looking saints repre-

46

36 Another fresco from the cycle of the Last Judgement in the Cathedral of the Assumption, showing Jacob, Isaac, and Abraham, this time painted in 1408 by Andrei Rublev and Daniel Chorny. These paintings clearly illustrate the stylistic changes which had taken place since Russia became converted to Christianity

sented on the Vladimir-Suzdalian icons is likewise absent from the wall-paintings, and so too are the decorative details which endow the former with an immensely sumptuous quality.

A deep love of decoration, though absent from the wall-paintings, lies at the basis of Vladimir-Suzdalian art. It inspired the superb damascene work carried out between 1222 and 1233 on the doors of the cathedral at Suzdal (*Ill. 37*). The doors are immensely heavy, being made of thick oak covered on the inside with sheets of iron and on the outside with damascened bronze. The west doors were adorned with twenty-four panels showing scenes from the Old Testament, whilst the south doors were devoted to themes associated with the Archangel Michael. The technique of fusing gold on to copper or bronze was a Byzantine one; it was quickly mastered

47

by skilled Russian metalworkers. The Suzdalian doors are of Russian workmanship. Some of their scenes, such as that showing Adam naming the animals, display a clear affinity with certain Yaroslavl paintings of late-sixteenth- or seventeenth-century date, and elements from both seem to be reflected in work produced today by the Palech workers in papiermâché. The magnificence of Suzdal's damascene doors may perhaps have aroused the jealousy of the Novgorodians and so led them to turn, as they did at much the same time to the West, to the metalworkers of Magdeburg for the embossed bronze doors of their own cathedral, though it already possessed a fine pair of damascene ones. Single panels from similar doors are preserved today in the Hermitage Museum at Leningrad, where their fine quality helps to suggest the extent of the loss suffered with the disappearance of the bulk of the country's early metalwork during the penurious years of the Mongol occupation. In those unproductive centuries metalworkers were fortunate if they were able to maintain their skill by producing such objects as iron bolts, locks, hinges, and similar utilitarian articles, as well as small metal amulets or objects of personal use, such as the combs the Russians wore attached to their belts by chains. They fashioned these lovingly, devoting as much care to their simple yet spirited designs as to their finish and workmanship.

37 A panel in damascene work showing Abel's sacrifice: the west damascened door of Suzdal Cathedral, 1222–33. The elegance of the work is typical of the Vladimir-Suzdalian school, but it is also a characteristic of Russian graphic art throughout the ages

The Novgorodian Period

In the tenth century Novgorod was perhaps even more important a city than Kiev; it was certainly as enterprising and as prosperous a one. It was there that Rurik had established his headquarters and it was only as a result of his death that Oleg, Regent and guardian of his young son Igor, was able to move the Court to Kiev, thereby making the latter city the capital of the Grand Duchy which took precedence over the other principalities. Yet if it fell to Kiev to tend the seed from which Russian culture was to grow and to Vladimir-Suzdal to endow it with elegance, it was at Novgorod that the national style was destined to evolve, there that Russian medieval architecture was to be fashioned and there that a school of religious painting was to develop, the products of which were often as rich and important as those of the Italian Primitives.

Novgorod appears to have been an autonomous city in 989 when Vladimir appointed Joachim of Chersonesus to become its first bishop and to act as supervisor of the construction of the thirteen-domed oak cathedral of Hagia Sophia. Yet within fifty years Yaroslav's son Vladimir was established in Novgorod as the city's reigning prince. Encouraged by Yaroslav, it was he who laid within the kremlin enclosure the foundation-stone of the cathedral of brick and stone which was to replace the wooden one which had been destroyed by fire. Begun in 1045, the second Hagia Sophia (*Ill. 39*) was intended to serve as the Novgorodian's principal church, and so to the last it remained, its fate being so closely linked with that of the townsmen that its role was shaped by the political changes which they brought about. Like Kiev's Hagia Sophia, the Cathedral of Novgorod was intended to serve both as the town's principal church and as the coronation church of its princes, and it was therefore provided with

38 (*above*) A marginal decoration from a sixteenth-century Gospel

a royal pew set in the centre of the west gallery; it was reached by means of a staircase placed in a tower constructed at the cathedral's north-western corner. As at Kiev the gallery containing the royal pew was extended along the building's southern and northern sides, and the church was given the cruciform plan and rectangular shape which had first been introduced to Russia at Kiev, but much of the resemblance between the two Hagia Sophias ends at this point. Thus, the Novgorodian church was built of undressed stone set in a pinkish cement instead of in alternating courses of brick and stone, though the arches above the doors and windows were still made of brick. Furthermore, the native taste which had dictated the thirteen domes of the wooden Hagia Sophia as well as of Kiev's masonry one was tempered in the stone cathedral by a more sophisticated, perhaps rather more Western outlook, so that only five domes rose above it and the number of its aisles was reduced to three. This restraint was extended almost to severity in the building's exterior. There the inspiration must have come largely from Chernigov for the effect it was intended to create was one of buoyant height and great forceful-ness. In order to stress the perpendicular character of the construction the drums supporting the domes were kept low, only the rounded lines of the protruding apses breaking the soaring spring of the walls. The interior of Novgorod's Hagia Sophia also presented a simplifica-tion of the earlier interior, striving after a plainness which accorded with the rather more dour, staid temperament of the Novgorodian merchants, who were the patrons of Novgorodian culture. The austerity was achieved partly by eschewing all use of such glittering, eye-catching materials as mosaic, partly by reducing the number of piers, and in consequence also that of the arches. The cathedral was completed by 1052, though its bell-tower was not added till the twelfth century, when the building also received the coat of white-wash on its outer walls, setting a precedent which was so widely followed throughout Russia that white-walled churches ultimately became a characteristic feature of the country's landscape. None of the wall-paintings which survived in the cathedral until their destruc-tion in the last war were contemporary with the structure; the earliest dated from 1108 and were carried out in flat paintwork unrelieved

50

39 The east end of the Cathedral of Hagia Sophia, Novgorod, 1045–52. It already displays such specifically Novgorodian features as the stressing of perpendicular lines, the absence of ornament, and the small number of windows. The sixth dome roofs an additional bay built later at the west end

by highlights, but notwithstanding the static effect which resulted from this, the scenes already displayed the vigour and forthrightness which were to become characteristic of the grander and more monumental Novgorodian style.

It was very soon after the completion of the stone cathedral that the Novgorodians determined to form themselves into a republic. Retaining their prince, but relegating him to a position of a military governor who assumed control only when called upon to do so, they ejected him from the kremlin enclosure, thereby depriving him both of his palace and of his right to regard Hagia Sophia as his royal chapel. The Prince and his household moved from the hill-top to establish themselves in the lower section of the town, and the Cathedral of Hagia Sophia automatically passed from royal ownership into that of the officiating bishop, whose importance henceforth may be compared to that of the Archbishop of York in medieval England.

In the course of the twelfth century the dispossessed princes founded two monasteries within easy reach of their new residence. The earliest of these was the Yuriev Monastery (*Ill. 40*). In the year 1119 the ruling prince engaged the Russian builder Peter to construct within the monastery's precincts the Church of St George, which was henceforth to replace for him and his heirs the Cathedral of Hagia Sophia in which he no longer enjoyed any privileges. Peter was a man of genius whose hand can be discerned in several important churches. In employing him the Prince may well have hoped to produce a church which would eclipse Hagia Sophia in beauty and importance. This was not to be, but the cathedral church of the Yuriev Monastery came to rank second in a district which was soon to become exceptionally rich in lovely churches. It was a building of considerable originality, for it already embodied most of the features which were to form the basis for the fully developed style of the fourteenth and fifteenth centuries. Thus the tendency to divide the outer face of the west wall into three vertical sections by means of stone or brick bands projecting some six inches from the surface, which had so far appeared only sporadically, was here extended to the south and north walls. The church was roofed by only three domes, but they too were to influence future architects, for by their asymmetric disposition they achieved a new effect, the picturesque quality of which later builders strove to attain. The shape of the domes shows that already at this date the transformation from the

40 The Church of St George in the Yuriev Monastery at Novgorod, built by the master builder Peter in 1119 for the Prince of Novgorod could never be mistaken for a Byzantine building so different is it both in its conception and proportions from anything that was being done at the time in Byzantium

squat Byzantine dome into the pointed Russian one was well under way, for although the onion-shaped contours which were better suited to the heavy snowfalls of Russia had yet to be achieved, the modification had begun, creating an outline which bears a strong resemblance to the shape of the helmets worn at that time by Russian soldiers. The drums supporting these domes, though they too had not yet assumed the tall, narrow, almost turret-like forms which characterize the Classical phase of architecture in the fourteenth and fifteenth centuries, already displayed, the decorative borders of triangular, dog-toothed, scalloped, and similar designs which appear in Vladimir-Suzdalian architecture and which were also to become typical of the Classical style. Most interesting of all, however, was the addition at the north-west corner of the church's west wall of a high, rectangular tower forming an integral part of the building rather than an addition to it. Within it was a staircase leading to the Prince's private pew and to the women's gallery. Externally, the tower's height and its oneness with the cathedral was emphasized by blind arcading, and here again, not only were the windows attractively disposed along the building's façade, but their long, narrow lines and rounded tops were also admirably attuned to its height and to the rhythm of its decorations. An attempt to reproduce the soaring, cube-like shape of the exterior within the church was responsible for the widening of the main aisles by the setting back of the inner piers—the asymmetric division which was formed thereby also eventually becoming generally accepted throughout Russia.

After completing the cathedral of the Yuriev Monastery the Novgorodian princes must have experienced some financial setbacks, for they do not appear to have built anything else till the year 1198, when they constructed the relatively small church at Nereditza. The great importance of this church to the historian resulted largely from the fact that the fine paintings which covered its inner walls were contemporary with the structure, and the total destruction of the church in the course of the last war is among the most serious losses suffered in the field of Russian art. Dedicated to the Saviour, the church epitomized to the full the Novgorodian contribution to art and architecture. On the outside, its north and south walls were divided into three unequal sections by means of flat strips of masonry, and at the same time the projections formed by the side apses on the east wall were considerably reduced to stress the importance of the main, central apse; but although the latter's width was thereby increased, its height was lowered. Inside the church the women's gallery rested on an oak balustrade, and the single dome was upheld by four square piers. A detached bell-tower of octagonal shape was added at the west end, a feature which future architects came to regard as almost essential. For all the charm of its architecture, the artistic importance of Nereditza largely depended upon its wall-paintings (*Ill. 41*). These were remarkable, both for their early date and because they survived practically in their entirety. Except for a broad strip of marbling running along the base of the walls, the whole interior was covered with biblical scenes which though executed, according to their pre-war restorer Myasoedov, by at least seven different artists working in slightly different styles, were all of exceptionally high quality. The painters had so much wall space to cover that the traditional scenes proved insufficient and others had to be evolved. As a result the paintings represented an important monument for students of iconography.

41 A general view of the interior of the Church of the Saviour, Nereditza, near Novgorod, photographed before the total destruction of the building in the course of the last war. Both the church and its frescoes dated from 1198; the paintings were of especially high quality

The traditional scenes occupied their customary places within the church. Thus, to give but a few examples, the Saviour looked down from the dome, the central apse displayed the Virgin Orans and also the Communion of the Apostles, and the Last Supper figured on the west wall. A portrait of the princely founder was also included in the decorations, justification for this existing in case of need at Kiev, but Myasoedov assigned the origins of some of the scenes, which were now making their first appearance in Russia, to places as far distant as Bethlehem. He also enumerated stylistic elements, the roots of which he traced to places as varied as Sinai, Syria, Salonica, the Constantinopolitan area, and even Western Europe. The presence here of so many diverse elements shows how varied Novgorod's contacts had become. The inclusion among the saints of the royal brothers Boris and Gleb is of historical interest since it represents their first known appearance in Russian iconography. According to the Lavrentiev chronicle of 1093, the Greek Metropolitan of the day had strongly resisted Russian efforts to secure the elevation of the murdered princes to the saintly hierarchy, and it was only when their bodies were transferred to the church which had been built for them at Vyshgorod by Izyaslav in the eleventh century, and in the course of the service the church became filled with a sweet fragrance, that the chastened Metropolitan agreed to Russian demands. Thereafter the brothers became a cult in Novgorodian lands, their memory being celebrated annually on 24 July, their representations being given a place of honour in Constantinople's Hagia Sophia (*Ill. 42*).

Now that the Nereditza frescoes are lost, our knowledge of twelfth-century Novgorodian painting depends on the murals in the church at Arguzhsk dating from 1189 and the remarkable ones in the church of the Mirozhsk Monastery at Novgorod's satellite city of Pskov. The latter are even earlier in date than were those at Nereditza and Arguzhsk; belonging to the year 1156, they adorn the walls of what is probably the earliest stone church in the district. As is to be expected in so much smaller and less prosperous a town than Novgorod, and one which had fewer contacts with the outer world, the Mirozhsk murals (*Ill. 43*) are both slightly more archaic and also more local in character than were those at Nereditza. But their high quality was a good augury for the future for, from the fourteenth to the sixteenth century, Pskov was to become the centre of a distinct, extremely forceful, and accomplished school of icon painting. Many of the characteristics inherent in the best of Pskov's icons were already present in the remarkable cycle of wall-paintings in the Mirozhsk Monastery, notably the artist's skill in spacing and composition and the monumental, almost Classical, sweep of his brush-stroke. The severe but deeply expressive faces in these paintings, the figures' taut limbs, their sombre, intense colour with stress laid on a dark olive green and an opaque red, the heavy modelling of the faces by means of much use of ochre and of white highlights, and the habit of outlining the features on the faces and the contours of the hands in a reddish-brown—all tend to create a deeply poignant impression: an atmosphere of heavy, almost oppressive silence.

The late thirteenth century marks a halt in Novgorod's cultural life. The Mongol conquest of virtually the whole of South-eastern

42 Icon of St Boris and St Gleb; a seventeenth-century work of the Stroganov school. The saints retained the popularity they had enjoyed in early medieval times throughout the Muscovite period. This elegant though late icon is adorned with a fine metal repoussé frame and haloes of contemporary date

Russia, and the efforts to extend this to include Novgorod, though averted, leaving the Novgorodians in control of their own affairs, nevertheless made it necessary for them to ensure their independence by the payment of a considerable yearly tribute. The Mongol threat was followed by a concerted Swedish, German, and Lithuanian attack which was only repelled when the Novgorodians had recourse to the brilliant generalship of their hereditary prince, Alexander Nevski. These trials inevitably affected the Novgorodian economy, the heavy expenses which had been incurred to secure the Republic's survival making it impossible for any building of importance to be undertaken. However, the fallow years were not wasted, for it was during this period that Novgorodian taste became fully formed under the influence of the forthright, practical merchants who constituted the bulk of the Republic's population. Their ability to deal with the political and economic difficulties which confronted them imbued them with the self-confidence that led them to speak of their city as 'Lord Novgorod the Great', and which enabled them to formulate their artistic views as well as to create what is often described as the Classical phase in medieval Russian architecture.

With the return of economic prosperity in the fourteenth century numerous churches were built in Novgorod, in Pskov, and in the outlying territories by people belonging to many different walks of

43 A detail from a fresco of the Lamentation in the church of the Mirozhsk Monastery, Pskov, 1156; it illustrates the rhythmical quality and profoundly emotional spirit of Pskovian painting

44 (*left*) The Church of St Nicholas, Lipna, Novgorod, built by Bishop Clement in 1292 is the first building in which the sloping roof replaced the flat one of Byzantine origin

45 (*right*) The Church of the Saviour, Iliina, Novgorod, 1372, dates from what is regarded as the Classical phase of Novgorodian architecture. The arcading on the apse may well be due to Western influence

life; as a result some churches were very large, others little more than tiny chapels. The new canons of taste appeared first in the small Church of St Nicholas on the Lipna at Novgorod (*Ill. 44*). Built in 1292 by Bishop Clement, it was adorned within a few years of its construction with fine mural paintings. Two new features distinguish its exterior from churches of pre-Mongol invasion date; the first is the introduction in it of the sloping roof, which was far better suited to the Russian climate than the vaulted Byzantine one, and which produced the attractive, inverted V-shaped pediment-like tops to the walls; the second consists in the elimination of the side apses and the linking of the pilasters dividing the outer walls into sections by means of scalloped or other forms of decorative masonry. It became customary at this period to surmount church domes with splendid if rather heavy crosses made of stout oak encased in a covering of lead or iron. The Pskovians were not imitators so that, although they evolved on similar lines as the Novgorodians, they did so independently; as a result, Pskov's churches contain features which are peculiar to themselves. Some of them even forestalled developments in Novgorod and Moscow, often by as much as a century. It was the Pskovians who reintroduced the side apses which the Novgorodians had abolished, and it was they who divided the outer walls of their churches into two instead of three sections. Their smaller resources led them to perfect the small church or chapel. Some of these were so tiny that, in the earlier phase, the piers supporting the domes' roofs occupied as much as half of the interior space; this obliged the Pskovians to resort to pendentives as supports for their domes, leading them to acquire such skill at this type of roofing that Moscow's rulers were often obliged to apply to them for experts, as in the case of the first cathedral church of the Troitse-Sergieva Lavra at Zagorsk. Another of Pskov's contributions to architecture took the form of the detached bell-tower as opposed to the belfries in which the bells had been slung between small piers or partitions. Most important of all, however, was the introduction of a porch-like exo-narthex known in Russia as a *trapeza*. Though there is archaeological evidence to suggest that the church on the River Nerl had been flanked by an exo-narthex it was at Pskov that the form was widely tried out in the twelfth century, when the addition to the main building first took the form of a rather elaborate stone lean-to added to both the west and north walls of the churches to afford much-needed shelter to worshippers coming from afar, who were often forced by bad weather to spend many hours within the church. The practical advantages afforded by these adjuncts were so obvious that Novgorod was soon adding them to its churches and the feature gradually became an integral one in those of late medieval date. It was in the fourteenth century that crypts made their appearance in the Novgorodian area; sometimes these were used as lower churches, often merely as storerooms.

Novgorod's livelihood and prosperity largely depended on the Republic's ability to maintain a flourishing trade. The Novgorodians were so well aware of this that they devoted most of their attention

46 The Church of St Theodore Stratelites, Novgorod, 1361–62, like that of the Saviour shown on *Ill. 45*, has the complex roofing, the three-fold division of the external walls, the heightened and decorated drum, and the helm-shaped dome which are characteristic of the period and the style

to this task, disregarding national as opposed to local political issues to the extent of dissociating themselves from Tver's attempts to raise an insurrection against the occupying Mongols. Even when Dmitri Donskoi, Prince of Moscow, managed to persuade many of the other reigning princes to join him in attacking the Mongols, an effort which led to the crushing defeat which Dmitri inflicted upon them in 1380 on the field of Kulikovo, the Novgorodians stood aloof. It was not until the 1470s, when Moscow had succeeded in moulding the other principalities into a single nation and had begun to turn her attention to the subjugation of Novgorod that the latter's complacency was shattered. Meanwhile, content in their seeming security, the Novgorodians devoted themselves throughout the fourteenth and most of the fifteenth century to refining the styles they had evolved. The embellished façade of the Church of St Theodore Stratelites (*Ill. 46*), built in Novgorod in 1361, is typical of their fully evolved architectural style.

Novgorodian painting did not lag behind its architecture. The importance attached to it as far back as the twelfth century is not only attested to by such major decorative works as the mural decorations of the churches of Nereditza and the Mirozhsk Monastery, but also by the quality and diversity of the illuminations with which they enriched their numerous manuscripts. The majority were religious in character, and the bulk of these were adorned with figures of the Evangelists bearing a close resemblance to their Byzantine prototypes, but Russian taste inspired the designs for the decorative chapterheads and tail-pieces, as well as for some marginal decorations, which were usually of a floral nature. The indigenous element appeared still more clearly in the forms which were evolved for the capital letters used at the start of a paragraph. Many of these were of secular character, showing Russian musicians playing their native instruments or men engaged on rural occupations, but others combined interlace patterns of Norse origin with animal attributes which, though derived from folk art, and thus from Scythian sources, also bear a resemblance to certain Celtic illuminations. However, the basic canons of the more traditional designs came to the Novgorodians from Byzantium by way of Kiev.

The strength of the bond linking Novgorod to Kiev and Byzantium is clearly to be seen in the oldest examples of Novgorodian icon painting that we know. Two of the earliest icons—a St George and a St Nicholas—are of twelfth-century date. The St George (*Ill. 49*) was only discovered in 1939 when his outlines were noticed on the reverse of a panel of the Virgin Hodegetria which had been brought for cleaning to the Restoration Workshops in Moscow from the Cathedral of the Assumption. The panel would appear to be one of those painted for the church of the Yuriev Monastery at Novgorod at the command of Andrei Bogolyubski's son Yuri, Prince of Novgorod until 1174, which were transferred to Moscow at the order of Ivan the Terrible. This is a noble icon in the Byzantine style, but the appearance of St George is markedly Russian, indeed essentially Novgorodian, in its solidity. Though his hair falls into neat, Byzantine coils which carry more than a hint of what may be regarded as Kiev's influence, and though the cast of his features remains Greek, Novgorodian forthrightness is responsible for the alert look in his eyes and the taut appearance of his body. Here is a soldier-saint accustomed to dealing with heretics and coping with worldly concerns, not an aloof patrician of Vladimir-Suzdalian origin, nor an ascetic Byzantine theoretician—nor a poetically conceived Sir Galahad. But there is more than a touch of Suzdalian influence in the inclusion in the picture of the symbolic sword of sovereignty; if the icon was indeed painted for a member of the princely house, the political implications underlying this small detail become scarcely less interesting than the panel's aesthetic value.

Towards the end of the twelfth century, Novgorod's contacts with Eastern Christendom became particularly strong partly as a result of the visit paid to Novgorod in 1186 by Alexius Comnenus, the nephew of the Emperor Manuel, and partly because it was becoming popular for devout Russians to undertake pilgrimages to Jerusalem, Constantinople, and more especially to Mount Athos. The custom had originated with Daniel the Superior, who set out on his travels in 1106–07, and who recorded his experiences in a work entitled *The Pilgrimage of the Superior Daniel to the Holy Land*. Widely talked of in its day, the work still makes fascinating reading. Contacts such as these resulted at the turn of the century in the production of some very fine icons. The one of St Nicholas (*Ill. 47*), which formerly belonged to the Novodevichi Monastery and which is now at the Tretyakov Gallery, heralds the series. It displays a half-length rendering of the Saint in the act of benediction. The centre of the upper margin is adorned with a throne symbolizing the Etimassia, the others, with full and half-length figures of Saints Cosmos, Damian, Gleb, Florus, Laurus, Paraskevi, Eudoxia, Fetunia, and Anastasius. The ascetic, anguished expression of St Nicholas's face and the use of highlights conform to Byzantine tradition, but the graphic handling of his hair and eyebrows, expressing the Russian interest in symmetrical, rhythmic composition, is a Novgorodian characteristic.

By the mid-fourteenth century the finest and most sophisticated icons combined a strong feeling for linear rhythm with a deeply emotional forcefulness of expression. This expressive element was largely achieved by means of deep modelling of the face, applied to

47 Icon of St Nicholas with saints in the margins; the figure of St Nicholas dates from the twelfth century, those of the saints from the thirteenth. According to tradition the icon was brought to Moscow by Ivan the Terrible and set up in the cathedral of the Novodevichi Monastery. The manner of presentation was adhered to throughout the centuries, but the austere, elongated rendering is characteristic of the Early Novgorodian school

produce heart-shaped cheekbones and to give the full, almost pursed lips a poignant look, as in the superb icon of The Saviour of the Fiery Eye (*Ill. 48*). To balance the lower part of the face, the fore-head and hair were often worked with rhythmical, undulating lines, whilst the eyes, which were depended upon for the culminating

48 Icon of The Saviour of the Fiery Eye; mid fourteenth century. The icon formerly belonged to the Cathedral of the Assumption in Moscow and is probably one of those commissioned by Ivan Kalita for the iconostasis of the first cathedral

49 Icon of St George; twelfth century. Though a Greek work it is one which was doubtless executed in Novgorod, or at any rate in accordance with Russian taste. It shows the warrior-saint holding his shield and lance in the manner which was popular in Russia, a Russian rendering of which can be seen on *Ill. 50.*

effect, were heavily shaded and underlined by regular, pulsating, curving lines.

Pskovian painting combined to the last a somewhat archaic manner of presentation with a taste for sombre expressiveness. Thus, the fine fifteenth-century icon of St Demetrius of Salonica (*Ill. 50*) retains the formal manner, frontal presentation, and static form belonging to the twelfth-century Byzantine icon of St George (*Ill. 49*), to which, indeed, it is closely related. However, the painting is more linear and at the same time less subtle, though just as monumental in character; the Saint's face is typically Pskovian in appearance, the highlight on the tip of his long nose being a characteristic feature of the style. Elements of folk art appear constantly in Pskovian painting: in this icon it is interesting to find the halo adorned with an interlace pattern of Varangian origin, which would have been out of date in sophisticated Novgorod, and to notice that his shield reproduces forms pertaining to contemporary metalwork.

СТЫИ · · ДМИТРЕИ ·

50 Icon of St Demetrius of Salonica; school of Pskov; mid fifteenth century. It
is interesting to compare this icon with the Greek one of St George illustrated on
Ill. 49, for it both closely resembles and yet distinctly differs from it

The Novgorodians were endowed with an exceptionally acute sense of colour and an innate understanding of its use. The paintings they produced scintillate like jewels, attracting even the most wayward eye to hold it entranced as it appraises with ever-growing delight the contrasts attained by the vivid, luminous tones which, for all their differences, harmonize without losing any of their forcefulness. Only early in the present century were artists of the World of Art group, and more especially those who were associated with Serge Diaghilev, to find inspiration in these icons which enabled them to produce equally glowing and seductive effects.

It may have been this feeling for colour and love of icons that led, early in the fourteenth century, to the introduction into churches of the iconostasis or screen separating the body of the church from the sanctuary, on which the icons were arranged in tiers in a carefully prescribed order (*Ill. 51*). The iconostasis may well have originated in the richly wooded areas around Novgorod where the inhabitants were fine carvers of wood. The innovation created a problem for the

52 Icon of the Crucifixion; a sixteenth-century painting of the Novgorodian school. The rectilinear lines of the building of contemporary style forming the background are used to provide a contrast with the curved lines of the figures in the foreground

icon painters, yet they quickly mastered it. There are usually three, and in the larger churches as many as five, tiers of icons in an iconostasis, the panels occupying the lower tiers being considerably larger in size than those on the upper ones. On entering a church the eye is instantly drawn to this vast expanse of painted pictures, the effect of which largely depends upon the immediate impression created by their tonal harmonies and linear rhythm. Yet it is not the general colour scheme nor the broad outlines of the composition that are alone important, for the nearer the worshipper draws to the iconostasis, the more essential does it become for the composition and colours of each of the icons to stand out in order to enable the individual panels to appear as distinct and separate paintings, capable of proving equally satisfying singly as in their prescribed sequence. On quite close examination it becomes imperative for each scene, each personage, each individual face to exercise its own magic, dispensing encouragement and comfort to each worshipper.

Novgorodian artists proved themselves fully able to fulfil these seemingly contradictory requirements and as a result they created a school of painting which is the chief glory of Russian pictorial art. They included in their range of subjects all the major iconographic scenes which had become traditional throughout the Greek-Orthodox world (*Ill. 52, 54*), but their practical attitude to life led them to become particularly devoted to the saints whose patronage was likely to prove especially helpful to them in their daily occupations. As many Novgorodians lived in remote clearings which were virtually isolated in the midst of vast forests, it was natural that they should not have broken altogether free from the old pagan conceptions, and that they should prefer saints who were the acknowledged patrons of particular trades or those whose intercessionary powers might preserve them from specific dangers. Thus Florus and Laurus, who were venerated as the patrons of horses and grooms, and Elias (*Ill. 53*), who was carried to heaven in a fiery chariot and so became the preserver from fire, were some of the more popular Novgorodian saints.

The Novgorodians' concern with realities did not prevent them from being keenly interested in intellectual pursuits. The vast majority were able to read and write, though they used birch bark instead of parchment or paper for their daily jottings. A very high proportion of their religious, scientific, and literary works were adorned with splendid illuminations, but it was only when Moscow's threat to their independence assumed dangerous proportions that their interest in history, and more particularly in their own past became profound. Their appreciation of ancient feats of valour is reflected in several of their icons, notably in that illustrating the battle which their ancestors fought in 1169 against the Suzdalians who were threatening Novgorod's independence (*Ill. 56*). At least three variants of this icon exist—one was formerly preserved in Novgorod's museum; another is in the Russian Museum at Leningrad. All are divided into three horizontal bands, each depicting a different phase of the battle. The two upper scenes show Ivan, Bishop of Novgorod, raising the famous icon of the Virgin of the Sign—the twelfth-century original is still to be seen in the Tretyakov Gallery at Moscow—as he advances at the head of the Novgorodian force to meet the invader when the icon's intercessionary powers enabled the attention of the Suzdalians to be distracted with the result that they were utterly defeated. Both armies are shown in full array, the soldiers in their panoply of war. The mass of contemporary detail is fascinating; equally exciting is the artist's superb use of colour, the fluency of his line, and the spirit of chivalry with which he has invested the scene. Although the composition is lacking in depth, it shows a definite feeling for life and movement, and its slightly archaic simplicity in no way detracts from the beauty of the rhythmical design.

The inclusion in this icon of contemporary costumes and other details of the same character may well have encouraged the introduction into icon painting of elements of folk-lore. These first appear in some of the marginal scenes belonging to biographical icons (*Ill. 55*)—more especially those painted in the district of Vologda—but it is in the somewhat later icons commemorating the founder saints of specific monasteries, in which the monastic buildings are faithfully reproduced without recourse to true perspective, that this element becomes dominant.

53 Icon of St Elias and the Fiery Chariot; a painting of the Novgorodian school, c. 1500. As the protector from fire St Elias is generally shown in Novgorodian painting against the radiant red ground achieved by using cinnabar which evokes the glow of flames

54 Icon of the Last Judgement; an early-seventeenth-century painting of the Novgorodian school. Whilst angels at the top of the painting unfurl a scroll, the Deesis cycle, with the Saviour isolated in a central medallion, forms the main scene. He is worshipped by angels, Apostles, saints, and three Patriarchs whilst a serpent coils up from the centre of Hell, where sinners and pagans are being subjected to suffering

55 Biographical icon of St Theodore; sixteenth century. An elegant, elongated figure of the Saint, shown holding the sword symbolizing sovereign power, occupies the centre of the panel whilst incidents from his life fill the margins, framing the central representations

Although the bulk of the Novgorodians were particularly fond of patron and biographical icons, as well as of those illustrating the Church's main festivals, members of the upper clergy and wealthier merchant class, both of whom had remained in constant touch with Byzantium, continued to prefer the grander, more austere icons of

73

the Byzantine type. Icons of this impressive and formal character therefore continued to be produced by the foremost artists of the day. The majority illustrate various iconographic versions of the Virgin and Child or of the Saviour.

The contacts which were maintained between Novgorod and Constantinople may have been partly responsible for bringing to Novgorod from his native Byzantium one of the greatest religious painters of the fourteenth century, a Greek called Theophanes. He arrived in about the year 1370. His remarkable genius and superb artistry emerge so clearly from the very small number of his works that survive that they suffice to place him in the forefront of his contemporaries. Though Greek by birth and outlook and, as Lazarev contends, assuredly Constantinopolitan in his artistic training, on settling in Novgorod Theophanes became subject to the process of change which was later so frequently to affect foreign artists working in Russia. As a result, although he has gone down in history as Theophanes the Greek, he nevertheless belongs quite as much to Russian art as his sixteenth-century countryman Theotocopoulos, who is also known as 'the Greek', does to Spain.

Like El Greco, Theophanes impressed all those who met him by his intellectual attainments. His knowledge of philosophy and his love of discussion made him renowned, but it was his artistic achievements which aroused the deep respect and admiration of the Russians.

According to Epiphanius, a contemporary Russian artist who got to know Theophanes well after the latter left Novgorod to settle in Moscow, the Greek painter was credited with the decoration of at least forty major churches prior to his arrival in the Russian capital. None of these is specifically named, but they are described as being situated in Constantinople, its Genoese suburb of Galata, and in Halcedon (Kadikoy) on the opposite side of the Sea of Marmara, as well as in Theodosia, Nizhni-Novgorod (Gorki), and Novgorod the Great in Russia. According to Epiphanius, Theophanes painted secular scenes and illuminations as well as religious mural decorations, on one occasion painting a mural decoration which included a panoramic view of Moscow on a wall of Novgorod's palace. For Epiphanius, Theophanes painted a miniature showing the Cathedral of Hagia

56 Icon of the battle fought between the Men of Suzdal and the Men of Novgorod; a mid-fifteenth-century painting of the Novgorodian school. This may be termed Russia's earliest historical painting; it is not without interest to compare its battle scene with the well-nigh contemporary paintings of Uccello

57 Detail from a fresco of St George from the *diakonikon* in the Church of St George at Staraya Ladoga, *c.* 1185. It is an astonishingly fluent rendering for so early a date and remote a region

Sophia in Constantinople with the figure of Justinian in the foreground, seated on a horse, holding a copper apple. The Russians were astonished by Theophanes' versatility, still more by his habit of painting from inspiration, without referring to tracings or manuals, conversing as he worked.

Novgorodian wall-paintings dating from the twelfth to the fifteenth century are as valuable aesthetically as the panel paintings, and almost as numerous (*Ill. 57*). Russian chroniclers associate Theophanes with the decoration of five Novgorodian churches, but of the paintings he produced there only those which he executed in 1378 in the Church of the Transfiguration survive. Lazarev draws attention to their strong resemblance to the superb rendering of the Harrowing of Hell in the *pareccleseion* of Kariye Cami in Istanbul of about 1310, and indeed there is much to support this view. In Novgorod, Theophanes' inspired, spontaneous method of working is reflected in the nervous, sweeping character of his brush-strokes as well as in his profuse use of highlights (*Ill. 58*). He moulded his draperies with the classic sweep characteristic of the Kariye Cami artist, and he gave his scenes colour schemes in which shades of

58 The central angel from a fresco depicting the Old Testament Trinity in the Church of the Transfiguration, Novgorod, by Theophanes the Greek, 1378. A fragment which illustrates the monumental character of Theophanes' work

violet and blue, and even silver, often predominate. The sophistication of his palette is matched by his skill in presenting his figures three-quarter face as well as frontally, endowing each with a vivid personality.

Though the closing years of Theophanes' life are linked with Moscow, where he died, and where his association with the young Russian monk Andrei Rublev was to prove significant, this period is less important to his own development than that which he spent in Novgorod. He was fully formed, and probably too old by the time he reached Moscow for that city to leave a mark on him. Comparison of Theophanes' Novgorodian work with the paintings in Kariye Cami at Istanbul, however, suggests that it was in the freer, more individualistic atmosphere of Novgorod that Theophanes' gifts as a great artist were enhanced by a more humanistic attitude to life than he would have achieved in fourteenth-century Constantinople. If he owed this keener response to the Russians, the Novgorodians in their turn were indebted to him for a better grasp of the technical problems connected with their craft. Indeed, Theophanes made so deep an impression upon them that many of the finest paintings which

59 Head of Abraham, detail from a fresco from the Church of the Assumption, Volotovo, *c.* 1380. Though more rustic in style, with features of the native Russian type replacing the Greek, the figures shown in these paintings are superbly dignified and profoundly convincing

were produced both in Novgorod and Moscow in the course of the fifteenth century reflect something of the Greek's metaphysical outlook in the elongation of their figures and the ascetic character of their postures, something of his imaginative range in the more subdued tones of their colours, as well as in the freer treatment of their drapery and their more complex compositions. Nevertheless, as the late-twelfth-century murals at Staraya Ladoga prove, Theophanes did not create Novgorodian painting any more than Novgorod created the art of Theophanes; rather, each made an impression on the other, thereby raising their respective achievements to a higher pitch than would have otherwise been reached. To assess both the extent and the limitation of Theophanes' influence on contemporary Novgorodian artists it is only necessary to compare the early above-mentioned murals at Staraya Ladoga (*Ill. 57*) to the equally important ones dating from 1370 to 1380 in the Church of the Assumption at Volotovo, near Novgorod (*Ill. 59*). Both series are essentially Russian creations; both retain clear links with the Nereditza paintings, but the Volotovo works acquired from Theophanes an alertness and mobility which endows them with an intense, deeply emotional vitality.

Indigenous Elements in Architecture
and the Minor Arts

It was in its wooden architecture that the Russian spirit expressed itself most forcefully, that its talent proved most articulate, and that the skill alike of its artists and artisans—who were often one and the same person—is to be seen at its greatest excellence. There were never any areas in European Russia in which wood was unobtainable; for the most part wood was cheap and smaller pieces often had no commercial value at all. Anyone who wished could find enough material with which to build himself a shelter, and there were always supplies at hand for smaller things such as furniture, carts, or horse trappings, all of which were usually elaborately decorated with carvings. For sculptures of a more precious character metals or semi-precious stones with morse, that is to say walrus tusk (*Ill. 60*), were also in general use in the extreme North. Such carvings were produced from very early times, and it is impossible to determine when the process of working wood first began; it must have been well established at any rate by the second millennium B.C. when the inhabitants of the bogland settlement of Gorbunovo in the Urals made a wooden scoop in the form of a duck (*Ill. 61*) of such accomplishment that the vessel cannot have been the first of its type to have been produced there. Nor was it by any means the last, for the form survived almost unaltered when made of wood (*Ill. 63*), and with only its contours attenuated when made of metal, to become the *kovsh* or handled wine-taster without which no Muscovite household was complete; indeed, wine-tasters of very much the same shape were still being made by the silversmiths of pre-Revolutionary Russia (*Ill. 62*).

Time, climatic disasters, and political upheavals have dealt particularly harshly with Russia's ancient relics in wood. Of the domestic architecture nothing survives that is earlier than the eighteenth century, of church architecture nothing that is older than the

60 A small writing-desk in the form of a casket with a *teremok*-shaped top. Made of pierced walrus ivory in the district of Archangel; early eighteenth century. Some of the plaques are stained green whilst the incised circles are stained black

sixteenth, and the number of objects of early medieval date to have come down to us is very small. Yet the wooden churches which existed in quite considerable numbers in Northern and Central Russia and in the Ukraine prior to the Revolution were among the most poetic of the country's monuments; all were redolent of the spirit which flows so exuberantly through Russian folk literature, inspiring all forms of folk art, and all must have reproduced building forms which had been in existence for a great many centuries. Even when found in a crumbling condition their decaying fabric acquired a nostalgic and appealing beauty which was given new life by the painters Chagall and Sudeikin (*Ill. 64*).

61 The prototype of the medieval *kovsh*—a wooden scoop of the 2nd millennium B.C. from the bogland settlement of Gorbunovo in the district of Sverdlovsk, carved in the shape of a wild duck

62 Silver *kovsh*, dated to 1635. By Muscovite times the *kovsh* has lost much of its resemblance to its original form in the hands of the metalworkers employed by well-to-do customers, yet it continued to retain the basic shape

63 (*below*) However, the animal origins of the form were never forgotten by the peasant craftsmen though they sometimes, as in the case of this eighteenth-century carved wooden *kovsh* of jug-like capacity, accompanied by its tiny ladle, resorted to animal instead of bird terminals

61

62

63

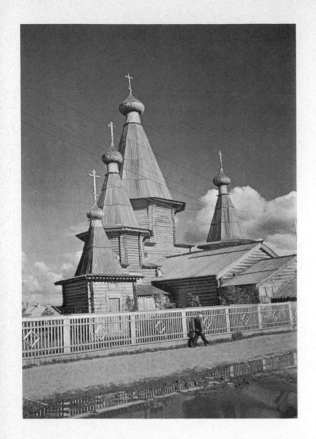

64 A wooden church at Kem, dated to 1714. Of the tent-shaped type, it clearly marks the three external divisions to which such churches were subjected. Its appearance is greatly enhanced by the preservation of the logs forming its outer walls, the nineteenth-century habit of encasing them in boards creating effects which were never intended by the original builders

Yet the great value of these wooden churches was not entirely dependent on the religious functions which they fulfilled, nor even on the aesthetic pleasure which they gave, but rather on the contribution they made to the development of Muscovite stone and brick architecture, for it was the native elements in their diverse styles which fired Moscow's imagination, inspiring the city to produce the most thoroughly Russian phase of Russian architecture.

The churches which induced the Muscovites to turn to indigenous sources for the salient features of their own ecclesiastical styles were of infinitely varied forms, but three in particular contributed far more to the formation of Moscow's later architecture than the others. None of the wooden structures which survived to our day could have been older than the sixteenth century, and many could date only from the beginning of the eighteenth. Their fabrics repro-

65 A wooden church at Suzdal; seventeenth century. A cellular type of church with a steeply pitched roof surmounted by a dome with the scaled surface that was so much admired in country districts

duced, however, the forms of infinitely older buildings. The innate conservatism of the Russian villagers no less than the country clergy's fierce opposition to any changes in either church construction or church ritual would never have permitted any deviation from the established type. Furthermore, it was only when a church had been completely destroyed by fire or some other calamity that it was rebuilt from its foundations; generally regular repairs were carried out on the existing building by the village carpenter, who replaced the worn-out sections with identical new ones so that it was not until the nineteenth century, when efforts were made to preserve the finer churches by encasing their log façades in boards as, for example, at Kizhi, Suzdal, or Podporozhie, that the appearance of some of them was altered by a change which, however regrettable, remained entirely superficial, and in no way structural.

Originally all the churches were built of logs, generally those of fir trees. In Early Christian times they were made into tiny chapels of either square, cottage-like shape or of octagonal plan. The buildings of this type which survived into modern times were devoid of aesthetic merit, but they served to reveal the origins of the three most important types of wooden churches. That known as the cellular, because it developed from rectangular, cottage-shaped sections, was particularly associated with Central Russia. In its earlier form it consisted of a fair-sized central compartment with smaller sections of similar shape abutting to its east and west ends. The eastern end formed the chancel and was roofed with a dome, the larger central section became the nave, whilst the western, which was separated from the body of the church by a wall pierced by only one small door, became the *trapeza* or hall in which people could shelter and, in case of need, even partake of refreshments. In later times the *trapeza* sometimes grew so large that it required from two to four columns to support its roof, but on the whole its dimensions, like those of the rest of the church, remained fairly small. With the years the three sections, though still retaining their boundaries, gradually assumed more attractive outlines till they eventually developed into buildings as arresting as the church at Suzdal, dated to the seventeenth century (*Ill. 65*). When the influence of the town began to penetrate to the villages and countrymen came to realize that the townsmen considered the top storey of their houses the best, they thought it only right to elevate God's house high above ground-level. Without in any way altering the external appearance of their churches they therefore introduced a series of ground-floor storerooms into the structure, thereby raising the body of the church to a first-floor level. This development obliged them to provide the church with a stair-case. This generally took the form of the external, covered staircase of Novgorodian domestic architecture, though its shape and disposition was skilfully varied to produce a pleasing effect.

Perhaps even more popular than the cellular type of church was that which, growing out of the octagonal chapel, evolved in Northern

66 The wooden Church of St Nicholas at Panilovo, 1600, contains a *kokoshnik* gable introduced in this instance to create a decorative effect. The external staircase with its sloping roof, though an adaptation from domestic architecture, was later to undergo considerable development in the hands of Moscow's architects, as in the case of the Church of the Ascension, Kolomenskoe, *Ill. 108*

Russia into what became known as the tent-church because its broad-based steeple recalled the shape of a tent. The majority of the churches of this type were fairly large, for the side sections of the octagons were eventually extended so as to provide the church with a cruciform interior. Internally, however, they still continued to be divided into three sections, the *trapeza* at the west end being separated from the body of the church by a wall having a small communicating door at its centre, whilst the large nave was divided from the chancel by the iconostasis which, as in most wooden churches, was often exquisitely carved and painted. The church at Panilovo, dated to 1600, is a good example of this type of building (*Ill. 66*).

In course of time in both Central Russia and the Ukraine steeples of the Panilovo type became the objects of elaboration, projecting sections being added to them at various levels with the result that

85

67 The Church of the Transfiguration, Kizhi, 1714;
though its log front was covered with boards in the
course of a nineteenth-century restoration nothing can
detract from its rhythmical and imaginative quality

they acquired an appearance which is strangely reminiscent of a
pagoda. However, it was the introduction, as at Kizhi (*Ill. 67*), of a
gable shaped rather like an ace of spades, though in fact it reproduced
the form of the *kokoshnik*, or women's head-dress of medieval
times, that was used to effect the transition from a rectangular or
octagonal base to the tent-shaped steeple. The gable eventually
became so popular that it formed a basic element of Muscovite
architecture, whether of wood or masonry.

In wooden buildings this *kokoshnik* gable was frequently also
used on churches belonging to the groups known respectively as the
cubic and the multiple domed. The first was a variant of the cellular
building, though in it the sections were cube-shaped instead of
rectangular, and compartments were often added to the sides of the
nave to produce a cruciform plan. The multiple-domed type of

68 The Church of the Trinity at Podporozhie in the district of Archangel, 1725–27, has also had its outer walls boarded over, but its roof provides the main interest. The cushion-like bases to its onion-shaped domes, all of which are scaled, were once a characteristic feature of the Russian landscape

church provided greater scope for the use of the *kokoshnik* gable. Its basic characteristic consisted of a group of five domes; these were placed above the central block. Later, when the number of domes was increased to seven, nine, eleven, seventeen, or even, as in the early-eighteenth-century church at Kizhi, to as many as twenty-two, different ways of disposing them were evolved. At Kizhi they are admirably combined with the *kokoshnik* gables which spring from the church's octagonal core, but it was more usual to see the domes rising, as at Podporozhie, dating from 1725 to 1727, from cellular or cubic foundations roofed by a sort of pyramid on a cushion-like base (*Ill. 68*). To lighten the outlines of such churches their domes were often give a scale-like surface whilst the circumference was slightly reduced. Each dome was surmounted by a cross whose elaborately shaped arms helped to sustain the decorative effect sought after by the intricate roofing. Internally pots were often built into the ceilings of the domes, but whether or not this was done to improve acoustics is not known.

Church bells had been unknown in Early Christian Russia, where the congregations were summoned to a service by means of a clapper, much as they are today in Greece and parts of Yugoslavia. It was only when the art of casting bells had been mastered that belfries and bell-towers began to be built, but neither of these reached the areas in which wooden church architecture was the rule until many years after they had become usual in the towns. When they did so they took the form of octagonal turrets which were generally placed at some distance from the west end of the church. The bells were mounted on to a small platform situated close to the top of the tower and covered by a diminutive tent-shaped roof.

Domestic architecture in wood has a longer history than the ecclesiastic. There can be little doubt that it had firmly established itself in Russia by late pagan times, for by then the major trading centres which had grown up at convenient points along the country's great waterways had developed into real little townships. Writing early in the tenth century, the Arabian traveller Ibn Fadlan noted with interest that the Russian merchants attending the trade fairs at Itil, the Khazar capital on the Lower Volga, used on arrival to set about building themselves a barn in which to live, and although they often used only a chopper as a tool, their skill was such that they invariably produced a structure of real architectural character. The references in early chronicles to the existence in pagan Kiev of at least three churches, one of which dated from 882, makes it abundantly clear that even at that date the town had become important, and that it must have possessed streets lined with houses, a square or two, and several temples. Elsewhere the poorer people were still living in partially sunken mud huts; they continued to do so indeed till well into the Christian period. However, excavations have shown that in the north of the country, notably at Staraya Ladoga, some log houses were being built in the seventh century. It is nevertheless hardly likely that Kiev possessed any buildings of great note before the middle of the ninth century, when early documents first mention

69 The Bukhtin and Aksakov's seventeenth-century house in Northern Russia was built according to principles which stretched far back into history, and which persisted in many a rural area till well into modern times

some. Even these were probably built of logs interlocking at the corners in much the same way as had been done in the fifth century B.C. by nomad tomb-builders of Scythian and kindred origins. Nor was this ancient method rapidly abandoned; indeed, it remained in use in modern times, not only for the construction of cottages, but occasionally also for the larger but less pretentious type of country house which was popular among the lesser gentry (*Ill. 69*). In early times the builders seem to have found it convenient to cut their logs to one length so that the oldest of the wooden dwellings must have been square in shape, but this practice need not necessarily have applied to the palaces of the earlier princes. All the buildings of early date appear to have been erected on oak foundations which, in the case of the larger structures, were strengthened at the corners by large blocks of stone. The poorer houses had floors of beaten earth, the better of wood. Glass, which was available from at any rate the turn of the ninth century, being used in Kiev at that time in large quantities for making into bracelets, was nevertheless so expensive that only the wealthy could afford to use it for glazing purposes;

70 Novgorod's kremlin and outer defences, with traces of the ancient *vallum*

poorer people had to make do with tiny openings in their walls which they closed by means of sliding, external shutters.

Early settlements were generally built on hill-tops, preferably those defended at any rate on one side by a steep bank with a river at its foot, best of all having as well a natural ditch on the other sides. Where natural declivities of this sort were lacking the inhabitants generally dug a ditch, where feasible, linking it to a river to form a moat. Vladimir encircled Kiev with a *vallum*, but by Yaroslav's day the town had spread eastward and it became necessary to extend the wall, which was then additionally strengthened with a ditch along its outer face and towers at its more vulnerable points. The earth walls were constructed in a manner which remained in use in Russia till well into the sixteenth century. The method consisted in building a spine of oak logs against which boulders and unbaked bricks were packed, the whole construction being bound together with clay and then buried beneath a great wall of earth, along the crest of which a palisade of oak logs of considerable height was erected as an additional safeguard. The walls which were built round Novgorod in 1044 must have been of this type (*Ill. 70*), as were those at Kiev into which, following Byzantine precedent, Yaroslav placed his famous Golden Gate of stone and brick. Only a fragment of one of its walls now survives, but a drawing by Abraham van Westervelt, showing it in the semi-ruined condition in which he found it when he visited

71 The Golden Gate at Vladimir; the pyramidal core was built by Andrei Bogolyubski in 1164 and the rounded bastions added in the eighteenth century. Andrei surmounted the gateway with a look-out post which he manned with men from his garrison, and topped the structure with a diminutive chapel. The gate faced westward, towards Moscow, then still no more than a small village

Kiev in 1651, reveals it to have been a triumphal arch of impressive proportions. Far more elaborate than Constantinople's Golden Gate, to which it bore little resemblance, it contained, set high above its pair of rounded archways, a diminutive chapel and a look-out post. A century later Andrei Bogolyubski, having decided to abandon Suzdal, where the nobles were antagonistic to him, and to make Vladimir Russia's capital, encircled the latter town with a wall pierced on its western face—the side facing Moscow—with a Golden Gate (*Ill. 71*), a Silver and a Wooden one being constructed at other points in the walls. Andrei's Golden Gate was a massive, cubic construction which survives today flanked by an oval, bastion-like projection of eighteenth-century date; from the start it too contained a diminutive chapel on its roof.

72 A great deal of jewellery was made in Kiev in pre-Mongol times. These cloisonné enamel pendants and necklace date from the eleventh to twelfth century, their secular decorations being of native origin

73 Carved walrus-bone comb of traditional form from Northern Russia; seventeenth century. The designs which adorn it can be paralleled in many wood-carvings produced in Central Russia, primarily as boat decorations

In early medieval times a town's most important buildings, that is to say its citadel, cathedral, and palace, were concentrated on the highest ground available and were safeguarded by an oak wall, forming the town's inner defence line. This complex developed into the kremlin enclosure of later times. Though the word kremlin is now generally automatically associated with Moscow, every regional capital originally possessed its own, and these remained in use throughout the Muscovite period. They had very much the same significance for the town's inhabitants as the Acropolis had for the ancient Athenians. The gates belonging to the kremlin walls were always important architecturally as well as symbolically. Today nothing survives of Kiev's kremlin, nor of the wooden or stone palaces in which the Kievan Grand Dukes held court, but many an old folk tale is set aglow by allusions to the turreted women's quarters, to the shining glass windows, to the great banqueting halls, and to the decorations in mosaics and paint which adorned their walls. There is reason to think that the earliest of these palaces was at least two storeys high, though it may well be that the ground floor

74 The face and obverse of a twelfth-century cloisonné enamel pendant on copper. The Saint's face is typically Greek, but the geometric decorations on the back of the pendant are characteristic of Russian designers

75 A cast and chiselled bronze aquamanile of thirteenth-century date. The bronze has been identified as an African cheetah, an animal which was used for hunting in Asia Minor

76 Two eleventh- to twelfth-century cloisonné enamel pendants, the one on gold, the other on electrum. The left pendant shows traces of Central Asian influences in its cloisonné designs, the ace of spade device frequently appearing on Seljukid objects of like date; the second pendant shows closer links with Byzantium

was entirely occupied by storerooms, as was the custom in somewhat later times, and as had been the case with the Greeks living in stone houses in the fifth century B.C. in Olbia, the Hellenistic city situated on the Bug and Dnieper estuary. In Vladimir's day the square in front of the Church of the Dime not only contained the four bronze horses which he had brought to Kiev from Chersonesus, but also a large, rectangular stone hall. It was situated to the north-east of the church and fulfilled the combined functions of throne-room, banqueting hall, and ward-room for Vladimir's bodyguard. Excavations have produced fragments of the paintings and the glass mosaics which once decorated its walls. The high standards set in pre-Christian times by Scythian and Sarmatian metalworkers and jewellers were maintained in Kiev in the Early Christian period, and there is good reason to think that jewellers' workshops were attached to the Grand Ducal palace; if so, the superb gold cloisonné enamels which are associated with Kiev (Ill. 72, 76) must have been made there, though the scarcely less fine enamels on a copper base may have been made by the equally skilled jewellers working in the town. Both were often decorated with bird or geometric motifs of Russian character, as well as with renderings of holy personages of Byzantine appearance (Ill. 74). Indeed, craftsmanship was so highly developed in Kiev that exquisite silver and gold vessels were produced for use in the cathedrals and the Grand Ducal palace, equally well-designed ones in copper or bronze being made in considerable numbers for the less wealthy (*Ill. 75*), and objects in iron for the poor. Toilet articles to suit every purse were also made (*Ill. 73*) as well as much rather rough, and a limited amount of fine quality pottery, but distressingly few earthenware objects of this early date have been preserved.

The earliest remains of a palace that survive are to be found at Bogolyubovo (*Ill. 77*) on the outskirts of Vladimir, where, from 1158 to 1165, Andrei Bogolyubski was engaged on building a residence for himself. Surrounded by a wall pierced by a Golden Gate, the compound contained a citadel, a cathedral, and a palace. The citadel stood on the highest ground at a point which overlooked the River Kliazma; it served as the pivot for the wall defences which were built of wood, strengthened at vulnerable points by stone. The cathedral stood beside the citadel, occupying a central position between it and the palace. Its interior may have resembled that of Chernigov Cathedral, for its roof was supported by columns surmounted by sculptured capitals. All four of its outer walls were decorated by a band of blind arcading set, in accordance with Vladimir-Suzdalian custom, at a fairly high level. The cathedral owed its most interesting architectural feature to its position midway between the citadel and the palace, for it was connected to them by covered stone galleries fitted into tall, ornate towers, one of which survives. There is reason to think that the palaces at Kiev and Chernigov were similarly linked to adjacent cathedrals, and that the churches at Kidersha, Pereyaslavl-Zalessk, and Nerl were also joined to abutting residences by similar towers, though these were built of wood instead of masonry. Excavations at Bogolyubovo have shown that the reception rooms of the palace were decorated with glazed tiles and gilt copper in addition to the customary wall-paintings; sculptures in the round were also found; many represent animal forms and came from the outside of the palace.

The destruction wrought in Novgorod during the last war has enabled the town to be more fully excavated than any other Russian city. Although, as Soviet scholars point out, Paris did not receive its

77 The tower which is all that survives of Andrei Bogolyubski's palace at Bogolyubovo, *c.* 1160. The adjoining covered gallery served to connect the palace to the cathedral. The treatment of the tower, with its Romanesque blind arcading and typically Russian flat archway breaking the essentially rectangular lines of the building, represents the only example of early domestic architecture in stone to survive. The steeple is of a later date, having been added when the building was transformed into the cathedral's bell-tower

first paved streets till 1184, Novgorod's had all been covered with roadways of oak laid across oak log foundations from as early as the eleventh century. When a section of this paving wore out, another was laid above it so that, in places, as many as nineteen layers have been found, the latest of which dates from the seventeenth century. Oak drains were also usual, and the town was provided with numerous public baths of the Russian type, for the Novgorodians regarded these establishments as essential amenities. The typical town house was a two-storeyed one, but its ground floor was entirely devoted to storage purpose, the living-quarters being concentrated on the top floor. These houses were probably roofed from quite an early date with the sloping roof which was later used to cover Novgorodian churches of the smaller type. Those belonging to the houses generally had a row of carved wooden animals or birds set along the ridge (*Ill. 78*), cocks and hens being especially popular figures; many of these retain a close resemblance to the cocks with which the nomads of Pazyryk in the Altai decorated their possessions in the fifth century B.C. The wooden gutters running along the sides of the roofs were supported by wooden brackets which were often finished off with very similar bird-head terminals.

Entrance to the houses was gained by means of an external staircase, which was often roofed over. This led into the large hall which occupied the central section of the house's first storey. It was often used as a banqueting hall; all the heated rooms which the family used throughout the winter were situated on one side of it and the unheated ones on the other; the latter served as summer sleeping-quarters for the family, and at all times as disrobing rooms for guests. Sometimes the extremities of a house were topped by an extra storey, giving them a turret-like appearance which was often emphasized by their tent-shaped roofs. These sections of the house were known as the *teremki* (singular *teremok*); the *teremok* was particularly liked, so that its form is often reproduced in the miniatures and also the morse, wooden, or metal caskets of the period. The more important houses were provided with a courtyard at their rear; it was here that the family's private chapel was to be found, and that stabling, store-rooms, larders, and other utilitarian offices were situated.

Although a palace was built for the Bishop of Novgorod within the kremlin compound after the reigning prince had been evicted from it, nothing survives of this early structure. The most important examples of Novgorodian domestic architecture thus date from the fifteenth century and consist of two buildings commissioned by Bishop Euphymius, an ardent patriot, who was bitterly opposed to Muscovite encroachments, and who was attracted by Western Europe. He is thought to have used German as well as Russian labour for the hall which he built in 1433 to serve as a chapter-house and banqueting chamber. It was a square, free-standing, three-storeyed

78 A reconstruction by M. V. Krasovski and B. D. Grekov of the type of roofing used in domestic architecture in medieval times. Note the survival of ancient animal forms and the similarity of the decoration on the eaves to nineteenth-century peasant cross-stitch embroidery

structure equipped with storerooms and servants' quarters, and is reputed to have had as many as thirty doors. The stone of which it was built was cut into facets and the rib-vaulted, rather Gothic-looking ceiling of its great hall rested on a single central pillar, so that the building bore a marked resemblance to the Palace of Facets which was erected in Moscow's Kremlin in 1487–91 by the Italian architects Marco Ruffo and Pietro Solario. In 1442 Euphymius started work on a stone archbishop's palace; sections of its east front survived till the last war. A far larger building than the chapter-house, it was nevertheless only two storeys high and contained six rooms on its main floor; all had barrel-vaulted ceilings. Indeed, in the larger stone houses built for Novgorodian notables such ceilings came to be regarded as essential supports for the floor above. Equally necessary to houses of this sort were the ground-floor storerooms which, in the case of a merchant's house, communicated directly with his offices situated on the first floor for, here again, only the top one was used as living-quarters. The stairs were built into the thickness of the outer walls, partly in order to save space, and partly to diminish the risk of fire, which was a constant danger to Russian towns since these continued to be largely built of wood till well into the eighteenth century. Iron shutters kept in place by strong iron hinges and either an iron front door or one made of oak and studded with iron were usual. The frequent addition of a moat spanned by one or more drawbridges completed the fortress-like appearance.

No complete example of a fortified mansion has survived, for Novgorod lost much of its individual character at its union with Moscow in 1478, but a number of old houses were still to be seen in Pskov earlier in this century. One of these, the Pogankiny Palaty (*Ill. 79*), gave a very clear impression of what houses of this type were like. Dating only from the sixteenth or early seventeenth century, it probably followed a far older prototype. Originally it consisted of a rectangular central block of two storeys, on to which two three-storeyed, rather longer rectangular wings abutted to enclose a large courtyard. The front of the house gave on to the courtyard, and the outer sides presented a grim, fortress-like appearance which was rendered still more forbidding by the absence of windows at street-level, for the storerooms which filled the entire ground floor were provided with windows only on the sides facing the courtyard. The house was entered from the courtyard by means of a covered external staircase which led directly to the main hall situated on the first floor. This hall extended to the whole height of the house and was roofed by great beams, whereas the other rooms had barrel-vaulted ceilings. Many of the rooms were provided with cupboards and niches cut into the thickness of the walls, as were also the lavatories, all of which were fitted with drains. Some rooms were floored with square blocks, giving an effect of parquet, others with boards. The house was covered with the traditional sloping roof and, like the rest of Pskov's old houses, its façade was kept absolutely plain. It was not until the middle of the fifteenth century, under the impact of Gothic Germany as well as of Italian influence reaching Pskov from Moscow, that window and door surrounds made their appearance, but these took the form of plain mouldings; the intricate carvings becoming a feature of Muscovite style were avoided.

79 The Pogankiny Palaty seen from the main, that is to say courtyard side; early seventeenth century. This mansion of a Pskov merchant-prince is typical of the style which prevailed throughout Novgorodian territory in late medieval times

The small palace which was built at Uglich in the latter part of the fifteenth century, and which is sometimes called Prince Dmitri's palace, though basically Novgorodian in style, contains strong traces of Muscovite influence. It is built of brick, the upper sections of the outer walls being covered with geometric designs carried out in ornamental brickwork. Some authorities ascribe this work to the influence of the Italian architects working in Moscow for Ivan III, and they therefore assign the building to about 1480; others regard the brickwork as an elaboration of Novgorodian church decoration, and in consequence date the palace some twenty years earlier, but since this is the first instance of surface decoration of this type the later dating would appear the more likely. The taste for effects of this sort was encouraged by Moscow, whence it spread throughout the neighbouring provinces (*Ill. 80*), where it retained its popularity till

Peter the Great's westernizing reforms introduced new aesthetic standards into even quite remote parts of the country. Perhaps the most attractive example of elaborate brick surface decoration is that which adorns the smaller tower in the walls of the Kirillo-Bielozersk Monastery (*Ill. 81, 82*). It dates from 1635.

Towers with tent-shaped turrets were also used to strengthen the walls protecting the monasteries which had been established in isolated situations, often close to Russia's borders. Though they generally contained a chapel they were primarily built as observation posts, for many of the monasteries were in real need of fortifications since they often had to serve as repositories for stores and goods of considerable value. Indeed, the larger of these foundations were expected to fulfil curiously varied duties. Unlike Byzantine monasteries, whose task it was to provide havens in which the devout could apply themselves to the salvation of their own souls, the larger Russian foundations (*Ill. 83*) had to meet a number of worldly needs in addition to fulfilling their religious functions. Many were thus expected to serve as schools, medical centres, and charitable institutions

80 (*left*) A seventeenth-century church in Novgorod, dedicated to St Theodore Stratelites, showing the increased use of decorative brickwork on the drums of these latter churches

81 (*right*) At the Kirillo-Bielozersk Monastery, 1635, decorative brickwork of a type which had first been seen in the palace at Uglich reached an immense degree of elaboration

for the people of the neighbourhood, and to provide refuge for those pursued by the law or a heartless master. In addition they had to form historians and chroniclers as well as to run workshops in which icon and mural painters could be trained, and scribes and illuminators taught their craft and employed, whilst nunneries produced the embroideresses whose skill was appreciated far beyond the borders of their native land. These manifold duties did not exempt the monasteries from having to pay taxes, and it was in order to meet such obligations that the religious foundations developed their own industries, such as that of salt production. Nor were the monasteries able to stand aloof in times of national peril, for if called upon they were bound to provide soldiers from among their lay brothers.

82 A defence tower of the Kirillo-Bielozersk Monastery. This octagonal tower, in contrast to less vulnerable sections of the walls, is entirely devoid of decoration. It is provided with a look-out post—the small chapel, ending in a tall spire, completing this superbly proportioned bastion

83 The cathedral church of the Vydubetsk Monastery. Within the walls, in the security of their defences, the monks constructed cathedral churches of great beauty and elegance, surrounding them with subsidiary churches and chapels, creating thereby superb complexes of steeples, spires, and domes

In addition the monasteries which were situated on the country's eastern and northern borders were expected to carry out both garrison and also missionary duties, whereas those established in the safe, more highly populated areas had often to fulfil the combined functions of an insurance company and old people's home by permitting laymen to purchase a life interest in the foundation. This entitled the purchaser either to draw a pension in his old age or to take up residence within the monastery, in either case also ensuring his right to burial within the monastery's grounds and to regular commemoration in certain of its church services.

Monasteries of this calibre must have had residential quarters that were as well designed and as carefully built as their churches and refectories, but no wooden examples have survived to give us an idea of their appearance, though there are many buildings in stone of this type. However, the outlines of some of the wooden ones are recorded in a number of most attractive monastic founder icons.

Because of the disappearance of all important examples of domestic architecture in wood the survival, if only in the form of a scale model and a number of contemporary drawings, of a remarkably picturesque example of Muscovite workmanship is particularly fortunate. The model has preserved for us the enchanting contours of the Palace of Kolomenskoe (*Ill. 84*), near Moscow, which was originally commissioned by Ivan I, Kalita. This structure was destroyed by fire in 1591, but it was quickly rebuilt, once again in wood in the tent-shaped style, to remain in regular use, undergoing repairs whenever necessary, till Peter the Great transferred the capital to St Petersburg. Then the old palace was abandoned and soon forgotten. When Catherine the Great visited Moscow in 1768 she was displeased with the accommodation provided for her use and determined to build a modern residence for herself. Whilst seeking a site she stumbled upon ruined Kolomenskoe. She was enchanted by its beauty, but, undeterred in her desire for a modern dwelling, she gave instructions for it to be pulled down and a new palace built on its site. However, she was sufficiently alive to the merits of Kolomenskoe's architecture to ensure that an exact model of the doomed building was made before demolition work on it had been put in hand. The old palace

84 The royal Palace of Kolomenskoe as seen in the eighteenth century. Built by Ivan I, Kalita, it served as a residence for the rulers of his dynasty and remained in use under the early Romanovs. Built of wood it consisted of a series of haphazardly added sections and wings, some of the seventeenth-century additions being built of brick substructures surmounted by living-quarters made of wood

disappeared, and Catherine died without replacing it, but the model survives as a record of all that was best in Russian medieval domestic architecture in wood. Its beauty, even on a diminutive scale, still enchants. Nor was Kolomenskoe in its day unique. The Stroganovs built a vast mansion for themselves at Solvychegodsk in the district of Perm in the same style. They were a family of merchant-princes who played a prominent part in Russian history, conquering Siberia for the Crown and establishing an icon-painting workshop which was responsible for the last flowering of the art. Some town houses also followed the model. All had the size and the same rambling, disordered beauty of the picturesque timbered mansions of Tudor England; all were redolent of the poetic spirit of medieval Russia, combining with the utmost felicity the pomp, imagery, cosiness, and, it must be admitted, also the repetitive elements which endow the literary works of the period with their individual, particularly engaging flavour.

85 The Ludogoshchinsk carved wooden cross, 1356. The importance of this fine object is all the greater since it is one of the few works of art to be dated exactly. Its numerous carvings are executed with great spirit and skill, if in a somewhat naïve style. This detail shows Samson and the lion

When, as a result of the country's westernization, the wood-workers found themselves debarred from building magnificent palaces such as Kolomenskoe or splendid churches such as Kizhi, they turned their attention to the decorative field, often producing work of such quality that it is difficult to decide whether the object should rank as a minor work of art or an example of folk art. Apart from the customary church furnishings—such as iconostases, crosses (*Ill. 85*), candlesticks, lecterns, and so forth—which had always had first call on the craftsman's skill, carvers and decorators henceforth concentrated on producing objects needed in the home, in addition to furniture (*Ill. 86, 87*), making numerous articles of tableware, looms, spinning-wheels, and toys, likewise decorating their houses with ornate window surrounds (*Ill. 90*) and balconies, embellishing their sledges and garden gates, and even the crosses in their cemeteries.

86 A carved and painted shuttle of nineteenth-century date. Its decorations combine scenes drawn from contemporary life and bird forms of very ancient origin. The sirin, the sweet singing-bird with a human face, in this case beguiles the weary traveller as he travels across the snow-covered countryside

87 Carved chair and wooden candlestick from Tikhvin, near Novgorod, seventeenth century. Until the eighteenth century all furniture was rustic in character, and much of that which was used both in cottages and large country houses remained so till well into modern times

88 (*below left*) Carving in high relief of a lion; late seventeenth or early eighteenth century. Work of this type was produced to decorate a large variety of objects; this design is a blend of Western and Eastern elements

89 (*below*) Incised and painted decoration on a loom; eighteenth century. The influence of the Turkish Lâleli period, which may have made itself felt in Russia by means of textiles or ceramics, accounts for stylization of the tulips, but the treatment of the whole clearly illustrates the Russian genius for graphic design

90 Carved window-frame from a cottage near Smolensk; eighteenth century

The designs they were fond of using included geometric patterns of symbolic origin, floral motifs, and Eastern-looking animals such as griffins, fabulous birds, or lions (*Ill. 88, 89*). Especially interesting decorations were evolved for the wooden stamps used for decorating the vast gingerbreads (*Ill. 91*) which it was customary to present on ceremonial occasions with designs especially devised for use at births, weddings, or funerals. Some of these display dense foliage from amidst which people, dogs, or other animals appear, but some present animal forms which have become so stylized that they have acquired geometric outlines very similar to those that are to be seen on certain very early Turkish carpets.

91 A carved wooden stamp from the district of Vologda; eighteenth century. The design was intended for a ceremonial gingerbread of considerable size. The largest gingerbreads on record were made to celebrate the birth of Peter the Great and weighed in the region of two hundred pounds, thus depending no less on the skill of the pastrycook than of the decorator

Novgorod was so self-centred a community that it took little notice of the cultural life of the less advanced and often troublesome inhabitants of the forest zones, and its ecclesiastical art and architecture were therefore but little influenced by the styles prevalent in the rural areas. Moscow began to have a broader outlook with Ivan I (1325–41), nicknamed Kalita or Money-Bags because, by making himself purse-bearer to the country's Mongol suzerain, he had amassed the necessary wealth to enable him to buy out sufficient Russian princes to induce the Great Khan to appoint him Grand Duke of Moscow. The title gave him precedence over all the remaining princes, and thus made his own territory the most important in the land. His wish to make Moscow the capital of a unified country was tacitly endorsed by the Metropolitan's decision in 1328 to transfer his see to that town from Vladimir. The Muscovites showed a similar appreciation of their Grand Duke's nationalist aspirations, and this led them to take an interest in their fellow-countrymen and to establish regular contacts with various native ethnic groups as well as with their foreign neighbours.

But the old capital of Vladimir continued to be so highly revered that, in the opening phase of Muscovite history, it was the stone churches of the older metropolis which served as the primary models for those of the new. No churches of this period survive in Moscow itself; the earliest to do so are now to be found in and around Zvenigorod, a small town to the west of the capital, where the cathedral followed the plan and broad outlines of the Vladimir-Suzdalian style, combining them with the sloping roof of Novgorodian origin. The cathedral church of the Savvino-Storozhevsk Monastery (*Ill. 92*) on the outskirts of the town, which was completed by 1407, and that founded at Zagorsk (*Ill. 93*) by the statesman-prelate St Sergius of Radonezh in his Monastery of the

92 The cathedral of the Savvino-Storozhevsk Monastery, Zvenigorod, 1405–07. This is one of the earliest known examples of Muscovite architecture and bears much the same relationship to later churches in this style as does the Church of St Nicholas, Lipna, Novgorod (*Ill. 44*) to the later, more ornate churches of Novgorod

Troitse-Sergieva Lavra adhered to the same principles. They set a precedent which was maintained in the grander type of church for well nigh a century, so that even Ivan III (1462–1505), though he brought a group of Italian architects to Moscow, insisted that the most eminent among them, Rodolfo Fioravanti, nicknamed by the Russians Aristotle because of his wide learning and varied abilities, should regard the Cathedral of the Assumption at Vladimir as the model for the cathedral of the same name which he was to build for him in the Kremlin to serve as the dynasty's coronation church.

In 1380 Dmitri Donskoi's victory over the Mongols on the field of Kulikovo, though failing to break the Mongol hold over Russia,

93 Chapel and refectory of the Troitse-Sergieva Lavra at Zagorsk; seventeenth century. Though founded by St Sergius of Radonezh in 1407 the monastery continued to grow with the passing decades, drawing monks and pilgrims from all over Russia. Its latest important additions date from the eighteenth century

nevertheless greatly weakened their control of the subjugated territories. The importance of the victory was quickly realized, and the joy the Russians experienced aroused an entirely new sense of patriotism. It reached its peak in 1472 when Ivan III's marriage to Sophia Paleologa, the Italian-educated niece of the last Emperor of Byzantium, enhanced Moscow's prestige to such an extent that a contemporary aptly described the new capital as the third Rome. The sense of nationhood which then bound what had recently been no more than a collection of semi-independent though associated principalities into a single kingdom led artists and architects to turn to native sources for much of their inspiration.

94 The Saviour, detail from a full-length icon from the Deesis tier of the Cathedral of the Annunciation, Moscow, by Theophanes the Greek, 1405. It is interesting to compare this painting both with the Russian painting of the Saviour, produced some fifty years earlier under Paleologue influence (*Ill. 48*) and more especially with Rublev's treatment of the same theme (*opposite*). Both icons are of much the same date, but Theophanes painted his towards the end of his long life which was, according to Lazarev, sometime between 1405 and 1415

To begin with, the new tendencies expressed themselves in the illuminations which were produced for the well-nigh contemporary accounts of the Battle of Kulikovo. Some of these are at times a trifle naïve, yet this does not detract from their charm whilst, to the art historian, illuminations of this type have a two-fold importance, for they serve to show what the secular, native style in painting was like, and also to reveal the origin of the historical illuminations which were produced in considerable numbers in Moscow throughout the late sixteenth and seventeenth centuries (*Ill. 96, 97*). However, the great impetus to pictorial art, especially in the religious field, must be ascribed to Theophanes the Greek, who had established himself

95 The Saviour, detail from a full-length icon from the Deesis tier of the Cathedral of Zvenigorod by Andrei Rublev; opening years of the fifteenth century. This work is redolent of Rublev's serenity, of his faith in the good things of life, of the mood of happy optimism which swept Muscovy after the Russian victory at Kulikovo

in Moscow at any rate by 1405, and who may well have moved there a year or two earlier. His influence made itself especially quickly felt in the capital largely perhaps because he was almost exclusively employed by members of the reigning house, first decorating the Church of the Virgin's Birth in the Kremlin for the wife of Dmitri Donskoi, then painting some superb secular scenes on the walls of the palace belonging to Ivan Kalita's nephew, Prince Andrei, but, above all, in adorning the Cathedral of the Annunciation in the Kremlin for the Grand Duke Vasili. He was engaged on the latter task in 1405 when, according to contemporary records, he was assisted by Prokhor of Gorodetz and Andrei Rublev. As Rublev's

Кнѧзѧ владимира андр̃екича поикъ стоитъ клѕѕѣ кры́ла́
пл̃л꙼кѕ꙼вꙗкъ ждетъ ѡ́сматѡ часа̀.

96 An illumination taken from an early-fifteenth-century manuscript of *Skazanie o Mamaevom Poboishche* (Tale of the bloody encounter with Mamai). It shows Prince Vladimir Andreevich and his troop setting out to give battle to the country's Tartar suzerain

ПОИ ЧГО. СХЗХ БОИ НИЄДИНА ЄЛАНЄСОТВОРИ РАВЪ
РОВЄ НЧГИ ОНИ ПРИД. ЛИМХТ ТА ЄО ДАРОВХ. НОСХДИТ
ПОПРАВДХ МОЄИ ИДАСЄОЧАЄТСА ЄХБАГРХШНЫ . ИПА
ПОИМХ БРАТА ЄВОЄ ИНЪА ВОЛОДИМЕРАЙДЄИМИТРОПОЛИТ

ИПОВХДАЄМХУ ИАИ ОХ ТИРХД ЛИТОХ ВСИИ ИОХ ЄРАЗА

ИНЪ ВЕЛИКИИ ДМИТРЕИ ПРИ ЗБРАТО ЄВОИ ПОПРЄЩ
КНОМХ МИТРОПОЛИТХ

97 Another illumination from the same manuscript showing Prince Dmitri
Donskoi setting out on the campaign which was to break the Tartar hold over
Russia. In accordance with the iconic convention the scene, though it took place
indoors, is presented outside the building in which the blessing was conferred

name is placed last of the three he must have been the youngest and least experienced of these master artists; indeed, he may well have been assisting Prokhor, who was probably his teacher. Owing to a later rebuilding of the cathedral nothing survives of these murals, but some of the icons in the Deesis tier of its iconostasis are ascribed to Theophanes (*Ill. 94*). Though their unusually large size and sweeping brush-strokes denote the experienced mural artist rather than the panel painter, these icons are amongst the world's finest, their deeply emotional asceticism being expressed within the firmly controlled idiom and the severity of line which Theophanes must surely have acquired, at least in part, from the Novgorodians.

Theophanes made a profound impression on his Muscovite contemporaries; he taught them the value of freedom of expression and the importance of responding to the dictates of inspiration; and Andrei Rublev, Russia's greatest religious painter, would seem to have been one of the first to respond to this teaching. Very little is known about Rublev's life. The Soviet authorities celebrated in 1960 the six hundredth anniversary of his birth, but it seems more probable that the painter was born almost a decade later. In any case he must have been old enough in 1380 to share in the general elation aroused by the Russian victory on the field of Kulikovo. A note of happiness pervades his works, transfusing even the tragic scenes from the Saviour's life. Rublev entered the Monastery of the Troitse-Sergieva Lavra as a monk, most likely early in his life. It was probably there that he became a pupil of Prokhor, and he must at the same time have come under the influence of the learned and sophisticated St Sergius of Radonezh, the founder, and at that time the Superior of the monastery. However, Rublev did not stay at Zagorsk, and though he was later to return there, he spent many of the intervening years as a monk of the Andronnikov Monastery, where he appears to have died in about the year 1430. Though Rublev must still have been fairly young in 1405, when he acted as junior assistant to Theophanes, three icons in the festival tier of the iconostasis of the Cathedral of the Annunciation are generally ascribed to him (*Ill. 98*); they are those of the Nativity, the Baptism, and the Transfiguration. In 1408 Rublev, this time assisted by his friend, the monk Daniel

98 Detail from the icon of the Nativity by Andrei Rublev or a close follower, 1405, formerly in the Cathedral of the Annunciation, Moscow. This scene shows the Three Kings riding to pay homage to the newly born Child

Chorny (*Ill. 100*), was engaged on the murals in the Cathedral of the Assumption (*Ill. 101*) at Vladimir, when he probably also produced his version of the icon of the *Virgin of Vladimir* as well as the superb icons in the iconostasis of the Church of the Savvino-Storozhevsk Monastery. In 1422 Rublev was asked to return to his former monastery at Zagorsk to redecorate the walls of the Cathedral of the Trinity which had had to be rebuilt following a fire, and it was

99 A detail from the icon of the Old Testament Trinity, by Andrei Rublev, painted between 1411 and 1422. The figure shows the angel on the left of the group of three. The icon is considered to be Rublev's masterpiece, painted in memory of his first Superior, St Sergius of Radonezh, who died in 1411

whilst he was engaged on this task that he painted his most famous icon, that of the Old Testament Trinity (*Ill. 99*), doing so in memory of his first Superior, St Sergius of Radonezh.

Though so little survives of Rublev's work, it suffices to establish him as one of the world's great artists. His unassuming, serene, profoundly devout personality radiates from his paintings (*Ill. 95*). His inner fire and artistic integrity are attested by the absence of all trace of the influence of even as powerful an artist as Theophanes, for it was in broadening his outlook and giving him assurance rather than in moulding his style that the Greek left his mark on Rublev.

100 Head of Abraham, detail from a fresco in the Cathedral of the Assumption at Vladimir, *c.* 1408, now ascribed to Daniel Chorny. This illustration is a detail of that shown on *Ill. 36.* Daniel Chorny, though older than Rublev, was his close friend and companion, often working if not as his assistant as a colleague

There is thus no trace in the latter's work of Theophanes' nervous, Impressionistic brush-strokes, of his contrast of light and shade, nor of his fondness for striking highlights. In Rublev's painting the delicacy of line is of such importance that it reduces the figure to a flat, silhouette-like outline which serves to stress the personage's unearthliness. Rublev's delicate yet sustained, superbly harmonious colour schemes emphasize this other-worldliness, whilst at the same time endowing the figures with the substantiality necessary to make them convincing. Rublev's skill in eliminating all unnecessary detail helps to focus attention on his deeply religious approach without,

101 Icon of Christ in Majesty, ascribed to Andrei Rublev and Daniel Chorny, *c.* 1408. Painted for the iconostasis of the Cathedral of the Assumption at Vladimir, the work is of such high quality that it is impossible to regard it as a school piece

however, unduly emphasizing it. The delicacy of his character and his hand alike helps to imbue Rublev's work with profound spirituality and grace, yet it is the fervour of his faith, expressed as it is with complete naturalness and a winning innocence, as well as his tenderness, untainted by sentimentality, which, with the support of his luminous, truly celestial colours, endow his works with immense forcefulness. Their influence is to be seen reflected in most of the finest paintings of the fifteenth century (*Ill. 102*), but although the superb illuminations of the Khitrovo Gospels, which are dated to the 1390s, have sometimes been ascribed to Rublev, Lazarev is surely right in associating the miniatures of the Four Evangelists with Theophanes the Greek and the other illustrations with Russian artists employed in the latter's workshop.

124

102 Detail from a fifteenth-century icon of the Dormition, school of Rublev. This enlargement of the figures of the two grieving saints is sufficiently close to Rublev's work to help to reveal the master's conception of religious painting

The Kremlin's churches form a microcosm of the building styles which prevailed throughout Muscovy till the end of the fifteenth century. Fioravanti took from 1475 to 1479 to complete his Cathedral of the Assumption (*Ill. 104*) for Ivan III, its resemblance to its Vladimir-Suzdalian prototype (*Ill. 103*) being clearly evident in its exterior. For the second of the Kremlin's churches Ivan and his son and successor Vasili III (1505–33) turned to the Milanese architect Alevisio Novi, asking him to replace the old Church of the Archangel Michael with a new one (*Ill. 105*), which was to serve as the burial-place for members of the royal family. Novi introduced in the building a cornice, the first of its kind to be seen in Russia, as well as other Renaissance features, such as capitals and small pediments enclosing fluted, semicircular niches, the shape of which was

103 The east and north fronts of the Cathedral of the Assumption, Vladimir, 1185–89, which Ivan III instructed the Italian architect Fioravanti to regard as a source of inspiration when designing the cathedral of the same name which he wished him to build in the Kremlin at Moscow

sufficiently in sympathy with that of the *kokoshnik* gable to blend with it. For his two smaller, rather more intimate churches Ivan III preferred to turn to his own people. His annexation of Novgorod, followed two years later (1480) by the overthrow of the Mongol yoke, enabled him to employ in Moscow architects from Pskov. These started by building in the Kremlin a new Cathedral of the Annunciation (1482–90) (*Ill. 106*) on the site of the old, to serve the royal family as its baptismal church. Though embodying many features pertaining to the style of Vladimir-Suzdal—notably the proportions of the drums supporting the domes and the bands of external blind arcading—this building represents the first attempt to

104 On the right, Fioravanti's interpretation of the Vladimir-Suzdalian style—
his Cathedral of the Assumption, Moscow, 1475–79. To the left, the Palace of
Facets, built 1487–91 by Marco Ruffo and Pietro Solario as a royal audience hall.
Beyond, the crosses of the Church of the Saviour behind the Golden Lattice

reproduce in masonry certain features of wooden architecture, such
as the *kokoshnik* gable. Close to this cathedral the Pskovians built
the exquisite little Cathedral of the Ordination (*Ill. 109*), begun in
1485 and completed within a year. In it, as in wooden domestic and
ecclesiastic buildings, the church's floor was set above a series of
storerooms, thus making an external staircase essential; *kokoshnik*
gables were used on the roof, but blank arcades terminate in Gothic
points instead of the rounded Russian form.

The tall bell-tower of Ivan Veliki (*Ill. 107*), built by the Italian
Marco Bono between 1532 and 1542, was the first structure within
the Kremlin to strike an entirely new architectural note, for though

105 The Cathedral of the Archangel Michael built by Alevisio Novi between 1505 and 1509. Constructed of brick, the cornice was made of white stone. The effect was considered pleasing and cornices were introduced into many churches built in provincial towns such as Rostov till the end of the sixteenth century

allied to the octagonal towers of native origin quite as much as to Italian ones, the Western device of recessing sections of the tower and adorning each with a cornice-like top was used in it for the first time. It was from then onwards that the steeple began to oust the dome in

106 Cathedral of the Annunciation, Moscow, 1482–90. Originally a small and intimate church roofed with three domes, it was enlarged by Ivan IV in 1564, when the superstructures were added to each corner; as each of these was roofed by a dome, two additional domes were added to the main roof to bring the total number up to the symbolic figure of nine

churches built in the Muscovite area, appearing there beside the *kokoshnik* gable, regardless of the difficulty of executing the latter in masonry. One of the earliest churches of this type (*Ill. 108*) was built in brick in 1532 close to the wooden Palace of Kolomenskoe by Vasili III, in gratitude for the birth of his long-awaited heir, the future Ivan IV, who was to go down in history as Ivan the Terrible (1533–84). In it the problem of reproducing the *kokoshnik* gable was cleverly overcome, the gable still being used for the functional purpose for which it was devised; at the same time the covered section of the exterior stairways belonging to domestic architecture was extended into a covered gallery which became an integral, extremely decorative feature of later churches built in the style of that of Kolomenskoe.

In 1547 Moscow was ravaged by a disastrous fire. A leading cleric, a monk of the Simonov Monastery called Sylvester, affirmed that the disaster was a punishment by God of the youthful Tsar, Ivan IV. By dint of reiteration Sylvester succeeded in convincing the Tsar of this and in persuading him to convene in the winter of 1550–51 a council with the object of examining the abuses which he considered had grown up within the Church. The findings of this assembly were presented to the Tsar in a document containing a hundred headings with the result that the council has gone down in history as that of the Stoglav, meaning a Hundred Chapters. The recommendations which it made were wide-sweeping and raised fierce dissensions in the capital. Meanwhile Sylvester's harsh treatment of the young Tsar had so affected his character that the stability of his mind became permanently impaired. Henceforth Ivan succumbed to fits of ungovernable fury, and an outbreak of rage inevitably resulted in acts of cruelty which were ruthlessly carried out at the Tsar's instigation by his bodyguard. The period became one of excesses of every kind: excesses whether of brutality, of pietistic zeal, of decoration in art, of individual wealth, and of dire poverty among the masses.

107 A general view of the Kremlin's cathedrals with, in the centre, the church bell-tower of Ivan Veliki. The latter was built by Marco Bono between 1532 and 1542 on the site of a fourteenth-century church, though the two top storeys were added in c. 1600

108 (*left*) Church of the Ascension, Kolomenskoe, 1532, in which the covered galleries, external staircases, tent-shaped steeples, and *kokoshnik* gables, characteristic of architecture in wood, were adapted to masonry

109 (*right*) Cathedral of the Ordination in the Kremlin at Moscow, built between 1485 and 1486 by masons from Pskov, with the Church of the Saviour behind the Golden Lattice, 1678, on the left

Among the first buildings to reflect this trend was the Cathedral of St Basil the Blessed (*Ill. 112*), built on the Red Square to commemorate the capture of Kazan. It was built between 1555 and 1560 by the Russian architects Postnik and Barma, who set out to combine in it the two traditional church styles, that is to say that of the Byzantine domed church and of the Russian tent-shaped one. They used as their source of inspiration the church which Ivan IV had built at Dyakovo (*Ill. 111*), near Kolomenskoe, in 1553–54 to celebrate the birth of his own ill-fated son Ivan.

110 (*above*) A detail showing the Baroque treatment of the façade of the Church of St Nicholas, Khamovniki, Moscow; seventeenth century

111 The Church of the Beheading of St John the Baptist at Dyakovo, near Moscow, 1553–54; another building in the Baroque style which may have served as the basis for the Church of St Basil the Blessed in the Red Square at Moscow

112 The Cathedral of St Basil the Blessed in the Red Square, Moscow, built by Postnik and Barma between 1555 and 1560 to commemorate the conquest of Kazan. The Tsar was so delighted with the building that he is said to have ordered the eyes of both architects to be put out in order that they should not be in a position to produce anything better

The plan of St Basil's took the form of a central church encircled by eight chapels, each of which commemorated a national feat of arms, and all of which were linked by passages and roofed with domes. This internal arrangement proved less successful in execution than the external design, for although the church strikes the modern eye as being too lavishly ornamented and too brightly coloured, its form is nevertheless well conceived, each section developing logically from the other to form a harmonious composition. The Tsar was so delighted with it that he is said to have given orders for both architects to have their eyes put out to prevent them from ever building anything to compare with it.

The love of ornamentation, which was partly innate, but was also fostered by the introduction of the Baroque style, was given free rein in the latter half of the sixteenth century. Baroque trends did not, however, reach Moscow direct from Western Europe, but came by way of Poland and the Ukraine, where they had already undergone local modifications. In Moscow, where they are to be seen at their most successful in some parish churches such as that of St Nicholas, Khamovniki (*Ill. 110*), they assumed yet another, this time typically Muscovite, form. Yet whilst gay and ornate churches such as these were being built life in the capital was being constantly disrupted by political upheavals. The troubles connected with the succession to the throne led to rioting, which developed into civil war. Poland, one of Russia's traditional enemies, took advantage of the situation to invade the country and march on the capital. A halt to the trials which the population had to endure did not occur till the election in 1613 of young Mikhail Romanov to the throne. Nevertheless, throughout the whole of the period of unrest intellectual and artistic life continued to flourish. The number of tent-shaped churches which were built then tended, however, to outnumber the domed ones. At first the Patriarch, for in 1588 the head of the Russian Church had been elevated by the Tsar to that supreme rank, had attached little importance to this trend, but in the middle of the seventeenth century the office was filled by Nikon. The new Patriarch was a staunch Graecophile and a passionate traditionalist. Every deviation from Byzantine precedent struck him as evil and the

113 (*left*) The Church of the Intercession of the Virgin, Fili, 1693, was designed by Peter the Great's maternal relations, the Naryshkins, in the Western style. It was the first church with rounded outer walls to be built in Russia

114 (*right*) The Church of the Virgin of the Sign, Dubrovitzy, built 1690–1704 by Prince Galitzin, follows a similar plan. It also introduced Western features, such as the use of statues as a form of roof decoration, to Russia

tent-shaped church roused his especial anger. By dint of perseverance he succeeded in obtaining an edict banning the steeple church and ordering a return to the domed one, five domes being recommended as the ideal number. Between 1656 and 1685 Nikon applied himself to building in the prescribed style the Church of the Twelve Apostles in the Kremlin at Moscow and another in the Monastery of the New Jerusalem at Istra, to serve as examples to architects.

Nikon's dogmatism proved unpopular among the people whilst his desire to prohibit all change met with opposition from those members of the upper classes whose business had taken them to Western Europe, where they had come to realize the extent to which Russia had lost ground during the stultifying centuries of Mongol rule. Among those who disapproved of Nikon's retrograde policy

115 Fresco of St George and St Demetrius of Salonica on the south-west column of the Cathedral of the Assumption, Moscow, 1508. It clearly reflects the influence of Dionysius. Yet close though it is to the master's style, it is painted in less delicate, far more vivid colours than he was in the habit of using, and the two saints have their feet firmly set on the ground instead of being poised on tip-toe

were the Naryshkins, relations of Peter the Great's on his mother's side, as well as his tutor, Prince Galitzin. They encouraged the young Prince from his early childhood to take an interest in Western achievements. In architecture their attitude was to some extent reflected in the ornate, sophisticated church which was built at Fili in 1693 (*Ill. 113*) as well as the more experimental one at Prince Galitizin's country estate of Dubrovitzy which took eleven years to complete. The latter was the first circular church to be built in Russia (*Ill. 114*), and the first to be decorated inside and out with

116 Interior of the Cathedral of the Assumption, Moscow, showing the chandeliers which illuminate the wall-paintings and the icons in the iconostasis, and reveal the splendour of the cathedral's interior

free-standing sculptures. In it Galitzin attempted to express his conception of architecture as a three-dimensional, plastic art rather than as a combination of flat, geometric shapes.

In painting, our knowledge of the work of the earlier period is largely dependent on the numerous murals (*Ill. 115, 116*) that exist, for relatively few Muscovite icons of the fourteenth and fifteenth centuries survived the fire of 1547. Among the works which escaped destruction are a number of paintings by Dionysius, another great Russian master, and the first layman who is known to have been a religious painter and to have run a large workshop on professional lines. Dionysius lived almost a century later than Rublev. The first of his recorded works, the murals in the Parfuntiev Monastery at Borovsk, some sixty miles to the south-west of Moscow, are dated to 1470; his death is ascribed to about the year 1505. Dionysius was a more ardent and turbulent, a more adventurous and intellectual painter than Rublev. He belonged to a more sophisticated age and,

137

as a layman, he was more of a professional artist than any monk could be, for he was free to devote himself entirely to his art. As a result his compositions are more adventurous and arresting than those of either Rublev or Theophanes, and his fondness for the extreme elongation of the human figure (*Ill. 117*)—devised perhaps to create an ethereal effect which his more wordly outlook made it difficult for him to achieve by other means—as well as for swirling drapery produced an exciting impression of movement, which was further emphasized by his profuse use of highlights. Indeed, Dionysius had a far more distinctive style than was customary at the time, and he had many followers both among the mural and panel painters as well as the book illuminators (*Ill. 118*).

The fire had left Moscow so denuded of icons that the Tsar was obliged to borrow some from other Russian towns. He turned especially to Novgorod, where the standards were highest, but the borrowed icons could only afford a temporary solution, and it became necessary to import painters, more especially from among the Novgorodians, to assist the Muscovites in rapidly replacing the destroyed panels. These artists were established in workshops founded for the purpose in the Palace of Arms at Moscow. Some of the icons produced at the time inevitably display a blend of Novgorodian and Muscovite trends, but Muscovite elements gradually came to predominate. The typical Muscovite icons of this period are of relatively small size; they often contain far more figures than formerly, the heads, hands, and feet of these personages being smaller than on earlier panels, their faces rounder and more Russian-looking, and the architectural backgrounds more elaborate and realistic (*Ill. 119*).

The substitution in the course of the sixteenth century of fine-quality paper in place of parchment enabled the illuminators to use thinner, more transparent and delicate paint, and thus to create colouristic compositions of the type which Rublev's art had made popular. The demand for illustrated books grew apace, and while religious works continued to be adorned with illuminations of the traditional Byzantine type combined with chapter-headings and tail-pieces in which the Russian genius for design is clearly apparent, historical, scientific, and literary works were enlivened by excellent illuminations carried out in a freer style and with a wealth of contemporary details. The decision to produce a royal chronicle requiring several thousands of illustrations was rendered possible by the introduction of the printing press to Moscow, but even so, it exceeded Moscow's resources, and once again Novgorodian artists had to be brought to the capital to assist.

Towards the end of the sixteenth century the impact made on the capital's artists by naturalistic woodcuts of Western origin led painters to wish to break away from the iconographic convention. Under Nikon's severe rule this was not possible so that the painters sought for distraction in evolving illustrations of far more abstract and more mystical biblical themes than already existed, painting them in darker, far less glowing colours. At the same time they began to express their growing interest in naturalistic art by experimenting with Western forms of perspective, some of them, more particularly artists in Yaroslavl, also introducing genre scenes into their religious compositions. Portraiture (*Ill. 121*) also began to act as a powerful attraction and, perhaps encouraged by the exchange of likenesses which had taken place rather earlier between Ivan the Terrible and Elizabeth of England, several eminent men ventured to risk incurring the anger of the clergy by having their features recorded in paint. Even Nikon could not resist doing so. The finished works were of a strongly iconic character, but the Church continued to be so firmly opposed even to these paintings that artists were obliged to continue to devote themselves to religious painting carried out in the iconographic tradition instead of in the naturalistic style of the etchings in Piscator's Bible, which many of them found fascinating.

Many of the best icon painters of this late date received their training in the workshops the Stroganovs had established at Solvychegodsk, their Perm estate. They became the originators of the miniaturist style known by the name of Stroganov after their first patrons, though they only evolved it when working for the Tsar and his Court in the royal workshops at the Palace of Arms. The style presents the last flowering of iconic art (*Ill. 120*). In place of deep emotion the artists substituted the finest artistry, devoting much attention to subsidiary details, whether of architecture, landscape, or costume,

117 Icon of the Archangel Gabriel from the Therapont Monastery by Dionysius. The treatment of the drapery creates an effect of movement yet avoids all hint of fussiness; the curves of the draperies, reflected as they are in the Archangel's wings, help in no small measure to produce the monumental effects which distinguish this master's work

118 Miniature of St Mark from a sixteenth-century Gospel; school of Dionysius. Dionysius' delicate treatment of a scene and his habit of elongating the human figure have been retained but, for all its beauty, something of the master's monumental quality is lacking

119 Icon of the Last Judgement; Muscovite school; late seventeenth century. It is
interesting to compare this icon with the contemporary Novgorodian rendering
of the same theme illustrated on *Ill. 54*, and to take note of the more crowded
effect and more sombre colouring favoured by the Muscovite school

141

120 Menology. Saints and religious festivals; late sixteenth to early seventeenth century. Icons of this type became popular in Moscow at the end of the sixteenth century under the influence of the Stroganov artists, who excelled at depicting a great many figures on a relatively small panel without creating an effect of over-crowding. See also *Ill. 42*

121 Portrait icon of Prince M. V. Skopin-Shuyski; Moscow school; first quarter
of the seventeenth century. The Prince's early death (1587–1610) was a sad loss for
his lively and inquiring mind led him to encourage reforms. The portrait originally
hung above his tomb in the Cathedral of the Archangel, Moscow

reproducing the most minute details with an almost Oriental
delicacy and grace. Icons by the hands of the leading masters—men
such as Simon Ushakov, Procopius Chirin (*Ill. 122*), or the Savins—
fall into a group which has marked temperamental affinities with
works as diverse as those created by Oriental miniaturists and ivory-
carvers, Renaissance jewellers, the Pre-Raphaelite painters, and the
exquisite trifles designed by Fabergé. Works such as these often
belong to the end of a cultural phase, and the icons of the Stroganov
and Palace of Arms workshops provide a glorious tail-piece to the
story of Russian icon painting, for although individual icons of
quality continued to be produced until quite recent times, the art
drew to a close with the end of the Muscovite Age.

122 Icon of Our Lady of Smolensk; an early-seventeenth-century painting of the
Stroganov school. Avinov is inclined to ascribe the panel to Procopius Chirin, and
the elegance of the work does indeed suggest the hand of the master

123 In 1491 Marco Ruffo built the Redeemer Gate to the Kremlin on the site of the original Frolov Gateway, the new portal continuing to serve as the main entrance to the Kremlin. In 1624–25 the English architect Christopher Galloway added the Gothic clock-tower, which the Russian craftsman Ogurtzev adapted to Russian taste

Throughout the whole of its existence as the capital of Russia, Moscow remained basically a wooden town. From the first it had been a walled one, with its Kremlin occupying the triangular hillock which is bounded on two sides by the Moscow and Neglinnaya rivers. Dmitri Donskoi had fortified the town with massive walls, but by Ivan III's day the introduction of fire-arms had rendered them almost valueless as deterrents, and it was for this reason that Ivan turned to Italy for architects capable of providing Moscow with effective, modern defences. Fioravanti and his colleagues spent from 1485 to 1495 building the walls and towers which still today encircle Moscow's Kremlin. For aesthetic reasons each of the three sides was treated as a separate entity, though all were castellated along the top and had gun emplacements on their towers. The main front faced the Red Square; at its centre Marco Ruffo built the Redeemer Gate in 1491, the base of which was surmounted in 1625 by the Englishman Christopher Galloway with a Gothic clock-tower (*Ill. 123*).

124 View of the south wall of Moscow's Kremlin showing some of its defence towers and cathedrals

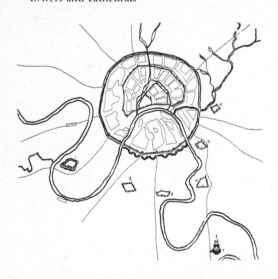

125 A map after A. I. Vlasiuk showing the triangular-shaped Kremlin at Moscow defended by an inner and outer ring of walls, with the fortress-monasteries forming advance defence posts. Seen from left to right the monasteries are the Novodevichi, the Don, the Danilov, the Simonov, the Novospasski, and the Andronnikov

126 The Novodevichi Monastery at Moscow was founded in 1524 by Vasili III to commemorate the liberation of Smolensk. The bell-tower dates from 1689 to 1690, the Cathedral of Smolensk from 1524 to 1525; the Church of the Trans-formation, seen on the right, from 1687 to 1688, and the Church of the Assumption, seen in the distance with the adjoining refectory, from 1685 to 1687

The Italians cut a canal faced with brick and white stone along the foot of this wall so that the water could form a moat along the length of the Red Square, a smaller canal being cut at the far end of the walls to link both rivers. There is no more Russian building than this Kremlin (*Ill. 124*), in spite of the fact that it was largely designed by foreigners; its gates, its towers, and its walls reflect in some strangely subtle way the spirit and troubles of medieval Moscow.

A belt of fortress-like monasteries served as an outer line of defences for the capital (*Ill. 125*). First came the Andronnikov Monastery, where Andrei Rublev spent much of his life, then the Novospasski, the Simonov, the Danilov, the Don, and the Novode-vichi (*Ill. 126*), whose lovely outlines still provide Moscow with one

147

of its principal glories. Within another century or so, however, Moscow had grown so large that the district of Kitai Gorod had grown up outside the walls, and in 1534 Petrok Maly was instructed to build defences round it; by 1586 the town had spread well beyond them, and Feodor Kon, the architect of the fine kremlin at Smolensk, was then called upon to build white stone walls to enclose the new district. Even so, in 1591, a Tartar army was able to break into Moscow and devastate the town. To ward against a similar occurrence a *vallum* of the old type was erected as yet another outer defence ring. By then the towers of the Kremlin's walls and gateways, with those of the other defences and the church steeples exceeded a hundred and twenty in number. Seen in conjunction with the mass of domes they led people to describe Moscow as 'the white walled, many steepled, many domed' city.

In 1691 Peter built a church dedicated to the Virgin of Vladimir in the district of Kitai Gorod. Though small in size, its destruction in recent times is to be regretted because it has deprived us of the first building with which his name is linked. On returning to Moscow in 1697 from his tour of Western Europe, Peter engaged Mikhail Shoglovin to build the Sukharev Tower to house a School of Navigation and Mathematics which the Tsar intended to establish. Shoglovin designed it in the tent-shaped style and Peter was so pleased with it that, in 1701, he commissioned a German architect to build an arsenal on similar lines. Far more interesting, however, was the Church of the Archangel Gabriel, built in 1705–07; because it was commissioned by Prince Menshikov it is often referred to as the Menshikov Tower (*Ill. 127*). Its architect I. P. Zarudnyi (died 1727) was born in the Ukraine, a region rich in wooden churches. As a steeple for the church he evolved a form which represents a blend of the many-storeyed wooden steeple and the recessed Muscovite tower, and he then proceeded to adorn the building's façade with door surrounds, balconies, and volutes covered with elaborate ornamentation in the Baroque style; these gave the church a wholly unprecedented secular appearance. Zarudnyi is the first Russian to have worked in a fully fledged Baroque style, and it is unfortunate that the spire of this church was so seriously damaged by fire in the

127 The Church of the Arch-angel Gabriel, Moscow, generally known as the Men-shikov Tower, because it was commissioned by Peter the Great's friend and most trusted minister, Prince Men-shikov. It was built by Zarudnyi between 1705 and 1707 in the Baroque style which Peter and his circle of friends especially admired

1770s that it had to be rebuilt. In addition to being an architect, Zarudnyi had his own workshops in which he employed a team of gilders and carvers. Peter so greatly admired their work that he commissioned from Zarudnyi the iconostasis for the church in the Fortress of St Peter and St Paul in St Petersburg and then placed Zarudnyi in charge of all the painters employed in the new capital, regardless of whether they worked in the traditional or the Western manner.

By 1703 Peter had become engrossed in creating St Petersburg and had lost interest in Moscow. Nevertheless, work in the older city continued, though it suffered a set-back in 1707 when Peter made Petersburg Russia's capital; in 1710 he issued a decree forbidding the use of stone and brick for building purposes anywhere outside the new capital. Ten years earlier Peter had abolished the patriarchate, reducing the head of the Church to his former rank of metropolitan,

128 The old Printing House, Moscow, built in 1679, but considerably restored in the latter part of the nineteenth century. With the palace at Kolomenskoe, *Ill. 84*, it was an inspiration to the medieval revival of the late nineteenth century. The Shchukin Museum, Moscow is a characteristic example of the revivalist style

and placing the direction of Church affairs in the hands of a synod. In 1712 this body in its turn struck a devastating blow to medieval architecture by prohibiting the construction of private chapels, an injunction which was extended in 1723 to include private churches on country estates. These laws, quite as much as the scale of the building programme being carried out in St Petersburg and the Sovereign's lack of interest in Moscow, brought to an end the medieval period of Russian architecture.

Only three domestic buildings of quality survive in Moscow from the medieval period. The earliest of these, the Palace of Facets, was built in the Kremlin by the Italians Marco Ruffo and Pietro Solario on lines which closely resemble both externally and internally the slightly earlier Novgorodian chapter-house. The second, the Terem

129 The Church of the Ordination, Donskaya Street, Moscow, 1701, is the last important church to have been built in the old capital before intensive building in masonry was confined to St Petersburg

Palace, though added to the Kremlin's buildings as late as 1635–36 by two Russian architects, Ogurtzev and Sharutin, to serve the Romanov rulers as their palace, is entirely medieval in conception. The third structure is the old Printing House (*Ill. 128*), which fulfilled the functions of a Stationery Office. It was built in 1679 in much the same style as the Terem Palace so that, although both buildings were considerably altered in the course of a nineteenth-century restoration, their proportions and general outlines remain redolent of the old city, giving us some idea of what its houses looked like before the majority disappeared in the great fire of 1812.

With Moscow's rise the minor arts came into their own again, equalling in quality and surpassing in their range all that had been achieved in Kiev in the pre-Mongol period. Technical developments led to great advances in the working of iron and copper; these were first reflected in the appearance of the crosses erected on the church domes and steeples (*Ill. 129*), the heavy crosses of the Novgorodian era being replaced by such delicately worked ones that their outlines assumed a lace-like quality when seen against the skyline. Iron and copper candlesticks (*Ill. 131*) designed for use in the churches as well as in the homes were given more spirited shapes and elaborate designs than formerly, and a variety of domestic utensils were made in copper instead of cheaper materials such as wood or rough pottery. More important still were the grilles made of wrought iron (*Ill. 132*); the finest of these, like the beautiful grille in the Kremlin and the equally fine one in the Novodevichi Monastery, being enhanced with gilding. At the same time the jewellers who, during the penurious years of the Mongol occupation, had only been able to produce church vessels and minor articles of personal adornment, were once again free to exercise their skill and ingenuity (*Ill. 133*). Using filigree, incised, embossed, niello, and enamel techniques, they produced a great variety of objects in silver, a considerable number of gold ones for the Court, and also gilt copper articles for the less wealthy. Chalices (*Ill. 130*) and censers (*Ill. 134, 135*) were required in considerable numbers for the numerous churches which were springing up throughout the country. Once again Gospels were being covered with gold or silver bindings embellished with inset jewels and enamelled plaques; once more icon covers and frames could be made of worked silver, gilt copper, and on occasions of gold, extremely delicate filigree work forming the greater part of their decorations, though some were embossed instead. For the first time for centuries not only the Sovereign, but also a number of his subjects could afford to own a variety of precious vessels. When in 1553 Christopher Chancellor, the Ambassador to Russia of Queen Elizabeth of England, attended a banquet in the Kremlin he was astounded by the quantity of gold plate he saw around him. It was at this period that the tsars began commissioning as gifts for those of their subjects whom they wished to honour loving-cups (*Ill. 138*), *kovshi* (wine-tasters) (*Ill. 136*), and goblets made of embossed silver adorned with niello, and often also with a dedicatory inscription.

130 A silver gilt chalice adorned with twelve polychrome enamel plaques which was presented in 1702 to the Metropolitan Samson of Archangel for use by himself and his successors in the see of Astrakhan for the Eucharist. Repoussé and open work provide additional decorations

131 These copper candlesticks of seventeenth-century date are characteristic of the metalwork which was being made in Russia in latter Muscovite times

132 Extremely delicate wrought-iron work was produced in Moscow and Yaroslavl throughout the seventeenth century. The gilt gates dated to 1670 in the Terem Palace, Moscow and the very similar ironwork at the Novodevichi Monastery, Moscow, are well known. This illustration is of yet another contemporary example

134, 135 (*right*) Though many secular objects were being created in the Muscovite period the output of religious vessels remained equally important. *134* is an ornate gold censer dated 1598, whilst *135* (*far right*) illustrates a silver censer dated 1597 which reproduces the tent-shaped steeple popular among architects of the period

133 Coconuts elaborately set in precious mounts were as popular in seventeenth-century Russia as in Western Europe. This late seventeenth-century example is set in a silver mount adorned with the type of Russian enamel work known as 'scan', which first became popular under Ivan IV

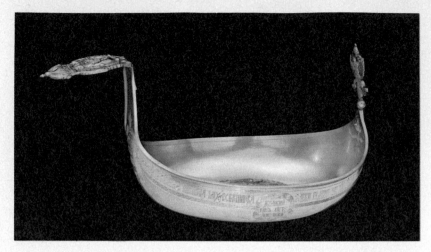

136 Under Peter the Great the *kovsh* became more angular in shape. Sovereigns often chose it as a presentation gift. The inscription on this one reads: 'In 1702 in December, the Great Lord Tsar and Grand Duke Peter Alexeevich presented this *kovsh* to the Novgorodian Mikhail Sereishikov for his devotion when he was burgomeister in the Liquor Tax Collection Department, and who collected as against the preceding year the sum of 18 thousand 920 rubles, 20 altyn and 2 tengi'

These articles became essential to every Muscovite household of standing, continuing to be so in Petersburgian days, when silver tableware first became general. Many of the later objects made in Moscow came to be decorated with garlands of Western origin and scrolls of Eastern character, relations with Italy on the one hand, and with Persia and beyond by way of Kazan on the other, having led to the indiscriminate employment in the Palace of Arms work-shops of Italian, Dutch, German, Turkish, Greek, Armenian, Persian, and even Indian craftsmen. The influence of the East was responsible for the production of vividly coloured enamel dishes (*Ill. 137*) and other objects, whose shapes retained their traditional lines, but whose designs represented a blend of ancient Russian, contemporary Muscovite, and also Persian motifs.

The Muscovites innate fondness for luxury helped to mould their taste and form their customs. Often their wishes could not be satisfied by the home market; often even the imports lacked the sumptuous appearance they desired. Thus, although finer quality stuffs had

156

137 A seventeenth-century silver bowl decorated inside and out with a floral design in enamel, the enamelled sections being edged with twisted silver to match the base and rim of the bowl. The choice of flowers is unusual for, as a result of Ottoman influence, tulips were generally shown by the enamellers

138 A silver bowl profusely decorated with niello work and an inscription referring to the donor, the Tsar Fedor, 1676–82

139 (*left*) Detail from a sixteenth-century embroidered chasuble; Muscovite workmanship. The design reveals Moscow's love of heraldry and floral motifs, as well as the extent to which its designers were influenced by Italy

140 (*right*) A wedding kerchief of eighteenth-century workmanship. The delicacy of the design is well matched by that of the workmanship

always to be imported, coming from Byzantium in earlier times, and from Italy, Turkey, and Persia later on, on reaching Russia their appearance was generally transformed by means of embroidery, plain materials being entirely covered in it, whilst patterned stuffs had their designs picked out in gold or silver thread offset with seed pearls and jewels. When under the impact, first of Byzantium, then of the Mongols, Russian women found themselves virtually confined to the living-quarters of their homes, being denied free access to the entire house, the more prosperous set up what amounted to veritable workshops within their *terems*. It was in these as well as in the larger nunneries that the superb religious embroideries (*Ill. 143*) which were renowned far outside the borders of Russia were made, the portrait shrouds of Moscow's noted divines (*Ill. 144*), the cloths on which icons were stood, and the robes of great prelates being worked in jewels, gold and silver thread, and delicately dyed silks and wool (*Ill. 139*). In the seventeenth century a *sakkos* made for the Patriarch Nikon weighed over twenty kilos. In the richer homes the maid-servants and their mistresses also embroidered the exquisite wedding

141 (*left*) A detail showing the back of a head-dress embroidered in gold thread. Yaroslavl work of the seventeenth century

142 (*right*) Detail from a gold and silver embroidery; seventeenth-century workmanship. The birds still retain a marked resemblance to those which figure in Scythian art

kerchiefs (*Ill. 140*) which were essential items of every bride's dowry. They threaded local seed pearls on to horsehair to decorate their *kokoshniki* (*Ill. 141*), and sometimes even fashioned the pearls into jewellery. Humbler folk, whose clothes were of felt or home-produced wool, spent their leisure in furnishing their houses with linen hangings (*Ill. 142*), cloths, and towels adorned with embroidered or drawn thread worked designs. Many of these continued to be reproduced in a but slightly modified form by peasants living early in our own century. Some of their designs display a marked resemblance to certain sculptures on the walls of twelfth-century Vladimir-Suzdalian churches as well as to even older prototypes, thereby linking the country's ancient decorative art to the folk art of pre-Revolutionary Russia.

So much has perished in Russia through the centuries that, today, the decorative art of the Muscovite Age has to be sought in folk art of, for the most part, a somewhat later date. Nothing is, however, to be learnt from it of Moscow's secular paintings for, on the whole, the peasants did not produce many paintings, possibly because of

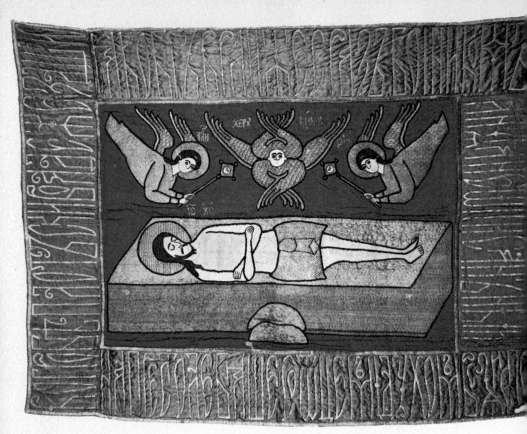

143 An early-seventeenth-century embroidered altar cloth of the type used to cover the chalice during Mass. The inscription is taken from a hymn sung during Holy Week and reads: 'In the tomb, in the body and in the heavens as God'

the relatively high cost and difficulty of obtaining colours. What painting they did produce dates from late medieval times and is generally in the form of decorations carried out on wooden objects as well as on glazed and unglazed pottery. Very little of the glazed pottery survives from the Early Christian period, and nothing of any aesthetic value appears to have been made during the centuries of Mongol domination. However, with Moscow's rise, Yaroslavl quickly developed into a flourishing centre for the manufacture of glazed tiles (*Ill. 145*). These display a rich variety of designs and are so enchanting that they were even sometimes used to form the external window surrounds which were an important feature of

144 The over-life-size embroidered portrait shroud of St Sergius of Radonezh, worked early in the fifteenth century in the women's quarters of one of the royal households, for the Prelate was both friend and adviser to the royal princes

145 An eighteenth-century Yaroslavl tile shows a young woman in Western dress, standing amid foliage and floral motives. The inscription reads: 'and I myself to my friend will go, and honey will I carry. . . .'

Muscovite architecture; the great majority were, however, produced as facings for the great stoves on which the Russians depended for their heating. It was likewise at this period that large, elaborate vessels such as jugs (*Ill. 146*) or acquamanili were made in glazed pottery in various areas of Central and Western Russia, and that rather coarse, painted clay toys in the form of figurines or of whistles of animal shape were made in great numbers; they retained their popularity among the people into modern times.

146 A seventeenth-century pottery jug from Rostov, the form of which reproduces that of a far earlier prototype. It still retains as a lip decoration the rosette which served originally as a symbol of the sun

Though members of Peter's household, and to a lesser extent his immediate predecessors on the throne, had paved the way towards westernization, no one had actually set foot on the road leading to it. Peter I (1682–1725) took the decisive step because he wished to retrieve at one stroke the two centuries of development lost to the country by the Mongol occupation. His policy made it necessary for him to insist upon changes which often represented a sharp break with the past, but he succeeded with remarkable speed in transforming a medieval country into a retarded, yet basically eighteenth-century one.

So far as architecture was concerned westernization was responsible for relegating church building to a secondary place, whilst the construction of administrative offices, palaces of up-to-date character, and smaller houses was set in the forefront. And, in much the same way as Vladimir had tried to catch up with the times some seven hundred years earlier by enlisting the aid of foreign specialists, so Peter looked to the West for the artists and technicians he required. But at the same time he took steps to ensure a future supply of qualified Russians by sending young men of promise to study abroad. He selected them from every walk of life, and many of his 'fledglings', as they were laughingly called, fully justified his choice, on returning home proving themselves a match for all but the most brilliant of the foreign architects.

The foreigners who had come to work in Russia had from the start to adjust themselves to Russian taste and Russian standards, especially to those of the reigning sovereign. Peter was himself a great admirer of things Dutch, and the site he chose for St Petersburg had much to remind him of the scenes which had charmed him in Holland. But though he was frequently carried away by these memories, he never forgot his visit to Versailles. The size of Louis XIV's palace, though

147 The church in the Fortress of St Peter and St Paul in St Petersburg, built by D. Tressini between 1714 and 1725. This was the first church of importance to have been constructed in the new capital. Originally its spire was more definitely Baroque in style, but it was destroyed by lightning in 1756 when the present, rather heavier superstructure was erected by the Dutchman Harman van Boles

148 (*right*) Peter the Great's Kunstkamera or Cabinet of Curios, St Petersburg, was built by the German architect G. J. Mattarnovi between 1718 and 1725. It now forms part of the USSR Academy of Sciences. Originally the tower was higher than it is at present

in essence less well suited to France's gentle, undulating landscape than to Russia's vast expanses, was equally important to both sovereigns as a symbol of power. As a result, although during the first half of his building activity Peter instinctively chose to be governed by Dutch sobriety, during the last ten years of it he allowed French magnificence to serve as his model.

To begin with, a certain amount of confusion arose concerning both the character and the exact siting of St Petersburg. The first foreign architect whom the Tsar employed, Domenico Tressini (1670–1734), came to Russia in 1703 and, with the help of I. Ustinov, started by building the citadel; it is known today as the Fortress of St Peter and St Paul (*Ill. 147*), and its gateway was the first example of the Palladian style to be set up in Russia. Louis XIV's death in 1715 enabled Peter the following year to procure the services of

149 A walk in the Summer Gardens with Peter's Summer Palace showing in the distance. The palace was built between 1711 and 1714, Peter himself making most of the panelling

Leblond, and it was to this experienced architect that the task of planning the new capital's layout was entrusted. Leblond's conception of St Petersburg was, however, very different from Peter's, for he thought of it as a defensive outpost, and he therefore sought to place it on St Basil's Island, situated on the north bank of the Neva, laying out its streets on rectangular lines somewhat reminiscent of New York's. In accordance with this plan the Court architect G. Schädel (1689–1752) began building a palace for the Tsar at Kronstadt and a far larger residence for Prince Menshikov on St Basil's Island, as well as another at Oranienbaum. When the Russian architect P. Eropkin took over the planning of St Petersburg at Leblond's death in 1719, he formed the opinion that the south bank of the Neva was more suitable for development than the north, both because it allowed for unlimited expansion and because, as part of the mainland, it would always remain in communication with the rest of the country, whilst the opposite shore would at times be cut off from it by floods. Building had by then already started on the south bank,

150 A water-colour by Alexander Benois, *c.* 1904, of the Hermitage Theatre built by Quarenghi between 1783 and 1785, and of the bridge connecting it to the Winter Palace. This evocative painting clearly shows the building's architectural features

for Korobov had begun the Admiralty on its present site, whilst the German architect Andreas Schlüter was engaged on completing the Summer Palace which Tressini had begun lower downstream, though Mattarnovi was at this time engaged on building Peter's Kunstkamera or Cabinet of Curios (*Ill. 148*) on the opposite shore.

Peter's Summer Palace (*Ill. 149*) was the first royal residence to be built outside Moscow since the construction of Kolomenskoe. To this it presented a complete antithesis for, however small, the new palace was a house of the West European and not of the native Russian type; it was in a style which, though inspired by Holland, was so very different from Dutch architecture of the same date that it is often described as 'Peter's Baroque'. With the years the capital developed on the south bank, as Eropkin had advised, but it

167

151 The fifth and last Winter Palace, St Petersburg, begun by Rastrelli in 1755 but not completed till 1817. Much of the final work was done by Rossi, though most of the capital's leading architects assisted at one time or another

centred round the Winter Palace (*Ill. 151*), which was from the start situated at some distance upstream from the Summer Palace in the vicinity of the Admiralty. The Winter Palace was to remain the main royal residence, but it was to undergo a number of transformations before reaching the form in which we know it today. The first version was built for Peter in 1711 to front on the Winter Canal; it was altered by Mattarnovi in about 1719, and again transformed by Tressini in 1725–26, when it was extended to cover the area occupied today by Quarenghi's Hermitage. It was in the completed section of this building that Peter died in 1725. Some time between 1732 and 1736 Rastrelli, though still a very young man, was entrusted with redesigning it. The version which he produced is known as the third Winter Palace; it had three fronts so that it faced the Neva, the

152 The cathedral of the Smolny Convent, St Petersburg, begun by Rastrelli in 1748 and virtually completed by him by 1764. The Empress Elizabeth intended to end her days in the convent, but died before withdrawing from the world, nor were the convent buildings completed to Rastrelli's design, though his model survives to record the original conception

Admiralty, and the Palace Square. Within a few years a fourth Winter Palace was set up by Rastrelli at the corner of the Moika and the Nevski Prospekt as a temporary structure of wood for use by the Court from 1755 to 1762 whilst he undertook the building of the fifth and last Winter Palace. This final version was only completed many years later to Rastrelli's design, S. I. Chevakinski (1713–c. 1770) and Y. M. Velten (1730–1801) carrying out much of the remaining work. In the 1780s I. Starov (1745–1808) and G. Quarenghi (1744–1817) took charge, the latter building the Hermitage Theatre

153 The Stroganov Palace, side facing the Moika canal, St Petersburg, built by Rastrelli, 1752–54, in which the vertical lines of the building receive greater stress than the horizontal

(*Ill. 150*), which he linked to the palace by a covered bridge. Further work was done between 1808 and 1817 by Rossi, who added the 1812 Gallery to the existing State rooms. However, in 1837 the palace was severely damaged by fire, and V. P. Stassov (1769–1848) was put in charge of repairs to the exterior whilst the architect A. P. Brüllov (1798–1877), a brother of the painter, was instructed to restore the damaged interiors to their original state. Yet notwithstanding the numerous alterations to the palace by so many different architects, the completed building is impregnated with Rastrelli's genius.

It was Rastrelli who created the fully developed Russian Baroque style which was to become characteristic not only of the Petersburgian area but of the grander buildings of the late eighteenth century throughout the whole country. From the start he gave his palaces an immense frontage, taking full advantage of the Russian ability to obtain striking effects from disposing numerous windows

154 The Cathedral of St Andrew at Kiev, built to designs made by Rastrelli in 1747. Following Muscovite tradition Rastrelli set the domes more widely apart than in the case of Smolny Cathedral

of uniform shape and size in rectangular lines; he used this severe background as a base for immensely varied, dynamic, sculptured, and architectural devices to produce ever-changing effects of light and shade. Rastrelli's remarkable genius was only equalled by his astonishing capacity for work for, between 1720 and 1763, quite apart from a variety of minor commissions, he built two wooden palaces in Moscow and a stone one at Rundal in Latvia, though he was building at the time a stone palace at Mitava for the Empress Anna's favourite, Count Biron, and reconstructing the Anichkov Palace, which Peter's fledgling M. Zemtsov (1688–1743) had built earlier in the century in the capital. From 1742 to 1749 he was engaged on building the Palace of Perovo near Moscow, yet in 1748 he had started on his lovely group of buildings for the Smolny Cathedral at St Petersburg (*Ill. 152*). Nevertheless, by 1752 he had completed his plans for the Palace of Pokrovskoe near Moscow, though he had been engaged since 1747 in enlarging Leblond's palace at Peterhof;

it was perhaps for this reason that Prince Vorontzov's palace in the capital took from 1743 to 1757 to build; Count Stroganov was luckier, for his only took from 1752 to 1754 (*Ill. 153*). It was when he was at his busiest, that is to say in 1747, that Rastrelli designed the lovely Cathedral of St Andrew at Kiev (*Ill. 154*), leaving the supervision of the construction to I. Michurin. The last decade of his active life was devoted to building the Winter Palace, which is his masterpiece, and the almost equally fine Catherine Palace at Tsarskoe Selo. Rastrelli retired to Mitava in 1762, but he did not spend his days there in idleness, for he turned his attention to the palaces he had built in that area when a young man, adding final touches to them.

Though St Petersburg is stamped with the imprint of Rastrelli's response to Elizabeth I's (1741–62) demands for elegance and ornamentation, the town is not wholly his creation. It acquired from its founder Peter its logical, rectilinear layout as well as the character of its streets, for many administrative buildings were constructed in Peter's day in accordance with his taste, and in addition it was Peter who drew up the specifications for the houses which he wished to see lining the streets of his capital. There were three types: the smaller houses were to have at least four windows fronting on to the street, the larger sixteen, and the biggest of all were to be two storeys high. In style all came to reflect the basic elements of the small Summer Palace which Tressini and Schlüter had built for the Tsar in his own version of the Dutch Baroque. The style was retained with but minor alterations for houses of this type almost until the time of Alexander I (1801–25), when they began to acquire the Empire look which remained with them till the end of the nineteenth century.

Catherine the Great's (1762–96) preference for the formality of Roman architecture in place of the exuberant Baroque which Elizabeth had loved is to be seen at its clearest in the palaces which were built for her on the capital's periphery, Cameron at Pavlovsk and Rinaldi at Oranienbaum being responsible for some of the finest work in this severe and impressive style. In St Petersburg, Quarenghi, Vallin de la Mothe, who worked in Russia from 1759 to 1775, Velten, and Starov evolved the Russian variant of the Roman order on lines remarkable for their purity. Quarenghi's Hermitage Theatre and

155 Entrance to New Holland, St Petersburg, by Baptist Michel Vallin de la Mothe; third quarter of the eighteenth century. Though the architect is better known for the Gostinny Dvor (Shopping Centre) which he built between 1761 and 1785, this lovely gateway is his masterpiece and a veritable architectural gem

Smolny Institute are masterpieces of their kind; the Tauride Palace, which Starov built between 1783 and 1788 as a gift from the Empress to Potyemkin to celebrate the latter's Crimean victories and to mark his elevation to the rank of prince, is almost as severe as these, and even grander, though marred by a slightly pretentious touch which is unusual in Russian buildings; most ardent of all is de la Mothe's work, his very handsome gateway over one of the Neva's subsidiary canals, known as the New Holland (*Ill. 155*), though often overlooked, deserving as much admiration as many of the town's larger and better known monuments. Its poetic note is sustained by the splendid sweep of the Neva's granite embankments and the elegance of the Summer Garden's railings, both of which were designed by Velten, and both of which contribute so much to the town's beauty.

Severity was to remain the guiding principle of Russian architecture throughout the late eighteenth and most of the nineteenth century, yet even in Catherine's day excursions into the extravagant were sometimes indulged in. V. I. Bazhenov (1737–99), perhaps the most gifted, and assuredly one of the most imaginative and least

156 The neo-Gothic bridge at Tsaritsyno Palace, by V. I. Bazhenov; late eighteenth century. Bazhenov was undoubtedly one of the world's least fortunate artists. Three times Catherine the Great entrusted him with commissions of outstanding importance, and on each occasion she cancelled the work. First Bazhenov was to have built an extension to the Smolny Institute, then a new palace in the Kremlin at Moscow, thirdly the Palace of Tsaritsyno, the structure of which was almost completed when the Empress abandoned the project

fortunate of architects, produced a Gothic conceit for Tsaritsyno (*Ill. 156*), the palace Catherine commissioned from him on the outskirts of Moscow and, when it was almost built, forbade him to complete. The Castle of Michael, which Paul I (1796–1801) instructed de la Mothe and A. F. Kokorinov to build for him at St Petersburg was a fantasy in a semi-Classical, semi-Baroque style, and during the reign of Alexander I, under the influence of Napoleon's Eastern campaigns, Alferov could not resist experimenting with the Egyptian style. However, whereas Catherine, her imagination fired by the discoveries of Pompeii, had looked no further than Italy for inspiration, Alexander I turned to Greece for his. A. D. Zakharov's (1761–1811) Admiralty (*Ill. 157*), which he began in 1806, but which was completed after his death to his design by Voronykhin, the architect of the Kazan Cathedral, in 1823, was in this severer style; it retained as one of its main features Korobov's original spire which

157 The main entrance to the Admiralty, St Petersburg, by Zakharov, 1806–23. The front of the building is over a quarter of a mile long, but the architect was able to give a false impression of its length by designing the monumental entrance set at its centre in the form of a massive pavilion

Zakharov now set on an arch the cubic proportions of which recall Novgorodian architecture. Notwithstanding its huge frontage and the massive appearance of its wings and entrances, Zakharov's Admiralty has a lyrical quality which is unique. Its rhythm is, however, to some extent reflected in the Stock Exchange (*Ill. 158*) standing on the Neva's opposite bank. The latter was designed by Thomas de Thomon in the form of a Greek temple. Thomon was a relatively inexperienced architect in 1801 when he submitted his plans for the Stock Exchange to the Commission of the Academy of Fine Arts, of which Zakharov was a senior member; they failed to satisfy the Commission and had, in fact, to undergo numerous alterations before their eventual acceptance in 1807, so that it is tempting to ascribe at any rate something of the poetic quality of the final design to the influence of Zakharov.

The final seal to Peter's creation was added by C. I. Rossi (1775–1849) under Nicholas I (1825–55). First he set off the beauty of the Winter Palace by enclosing a huge area on its inland front within the vast, sweeping, gently curving blocks designed to house the offices of the General Staff (*Ill. 159*). Though Rastrelli's palace and Rossi's War Office blocks are in completely different styles, Rossi succeeded in making his own plain but superbly proportioned structures blend admirably with Rastrelli's exuberant frontage, doing so by centring attention on the vast archway placed in the middle of the War Office blocks to connect the Palace Square to the town's main thoroughfare, the Nevski Prospekt; then by shifting attention back from the archway to the centre of the square, where he placed an immensely tall and slender monolith designed by Montferrand as a memorial to Alexander I, Rossi added the final touch of beauty to the Winter Palace and Admiralty group of buildings by designing as a background and terminal-point the splendid Synod and Senate offices. To the east of the Winter Palace he also built the Michael Palace, now the Russian Museum, in an equally severe style, but it is as the designer of the theatre which in his day was called after Alexander I, and the street leading up to it, that he reached the summit of his achievements. Originally known as Theatre Street (*Ill. 160*), but renamed today Rossi Street in his honour, the buildings which line it were built to house the Imperial Ballet School on one side of the street and administrative offices on the other. Both blocks are identical, but the grandeur of their severe outlines, the excellence of their proportions, and the rhythm established by their windows invests them with the qualities of a single masterpiece.

Just as Moscow had been surrounded by a belt of monasteries so, if unconsciously, did St Petersburg find itself from the start encircled by a chain of royal palaces. Schädel, assisted by Fontana, had been the first to build a palace. Begun for Prince Menshikov in 1714 and known as Oranienbaum (*Ill. 163*), it reverted to the Crown at the

158 The Stock Exchange, St Petersburg, by Thomas de Thomon, was inspired by the Temple of Poseidon at Paestum, but the architect succeeded admirably in attuning the proportions of his building to the vast sweep of the Neva

159 The Palace Square with the monument to Alexander I and the buildings of the General Staff seen from the roof of the Winter Palace, St Petersburg. Rossi displayed a faultless sense of proportion when designing the offices of the General Staff. The great gateway at their centre ranks with the finest buildings in the Classical style

160 Theatre Street, St Petersburg, by C. Rossi. Each side of the street is devised as a single block reflecting the one opposite to it. The architect relied on the rounded arches of the lower storey and the row of double columns above them to produce a rhythmical effect. This is maintained by the pilaster strips decorating the theatre which forms the street's terminal-point

161 The main cascade at Peterhof, designed by Leblond and completed by
Rastrelli. At the centre, the Samson Fountain throws a jet which reached a height
of sixty-five feet

Prince's fall from grace. Little survives of the original structure, for
the palace of the same name which now occupies the site was rebuilt
by A. Rinaldi (c. 1710–94) for Catherine the Great in the last
quarter of the eighteenth century. An imposing building with a
fine Neo-classical façade, the austerity of its exterior is belied by the
light-hearted decorations in the Chinese style in some of its State
apartments (*Ill. 164*).

Whilst Schädel was occupied at Oranienbaum, Leblond had begun
to build at Peterhof a large palace, which Peter wished to be the
equal of Versailles, as well as the smaller, more intimate residence of
Mon Plaisir in its park, on the edge of the Gulf of Finland. The little
that Leblond was able to accomplish before his death in the larger
palace was carefully preserved by Rastrelli, who flanked it with
wings of his own design, endowing the long, low structure with
such unity and elegance that the palace compares more than favour-
ably with Versailles. Indeed, Peterhof's water garden (*Ill. 161*) is

178

162 The Cameron Gallery at Tsarskoe Selo by C. Cameron, built between 1783 and 1785. The colonnade which the Empress named after her architect because she was so delighted by it, was designed to contain the busts of the ancient philosophers whom Catherine the Great especially admired, but she included amongst them the bust of Fox

among the world's finest, whilst the magnificence of the decorations and fittings designed by Rastrelli for the interior of Peterhof was equally hard to rival. The palace was virtually destroyed in the course of the last war, and although restored with astonishing skill, something of its beauty seems to have departed from it; yet it still remains outstanding. Leblond's central block is rather wider than Rastrelli's long and elegant wings; these terminate in pavilions which serve to balance the central section; one contained the royal chapel and was roofed by Rastrelli with the five domes prescribed by tradition, but endowed by him with peculiar grace. So successfully are the various sections of the palace linked and blended that it is difficult to dissociate them and study them singly; to appreciate the quality of Leblond's work it is, therefore, preferable to turn to the tiny Palace of Mon Plaisir as well as to the exquisite pavilions of Marli and the Hermitage standing in the park; their style is a blend of Peter's Baroque and France's grander manner which loses none of its beauty

on this diminutive scale; indeed, it serves to stress the delicacy of their outlines and to attune the restrained decorations of their façades to the idyllic settings afforded by the park. Peter was especially fond of Marli, where he could sit watching his fleet shimmering in the distance at Kronstadt.

At Peterhof, Rastrelli subjected himself to considerable restraint in order to ensure that his additions to the palace would blend with the rather more sedate style of Leblond. In Catherine's palace at Tsarskoe Selo he gave free rein to his inventiveness, designing a central block (*Ill. 165*), measuring some two hundred and twenty yards in length, and flanking it by vast wings which help to form an immense court of honour. Instead of breaking this huge mass into blocks, Rastrelli achieved both unity and diversity by means of similar repetitive effects of light and shade created by means of columns

163 (*above*) The Palace of Oranienbaum built by Rinaldi at the end of the eighteenth century. Much of the interior was decorated in the Rococo style of European Chinoiserie

164 The Toboggan Hill in the park at Oranienbaum by Rinaldi. Its mechanism and chutes have perished, but the building's severe façade and excellent proportions reflect Rinaldi's taste far better than does the large palace

165 The central portion of the main front of the Catherine Palace at Tsarskoe Selo built by Rastrelli between 1749 and 1756 once again displays the architect's skill in breaking up immense horizontal surfaces by drawing the eye upwards

grouped in different ways and combined with lintels of diverse types as well as with windows, pediments, and caryatids which, for all their superficial similarity, vary in their details. The treatment of the façade is in fact very close to that which he evolved for the Winter Palace, and it is the vast, rectilinear outlines of both buildings and the repetition of the basic elements forming their decorations, combined with their ever-changing details which make both so entirely different from anything that was built by architects working in Western Europe in the Baroque style. Later the Scottish architect Charles Cameron was to incorporate into an unfinished wing of Rastrelli's palace a series of private apartments and a covered walk for Catherine the Great, which so delighted the Empress that she called the latter the Cameron Gallery (*Ill. 162*) after its architect. The private apartments contained, till their destruction in the last war, rooms so perfectly proportioned, so imaginatively decorated, and so exquisitely appointed that they bear a closer resemblance to the creation of one of Catherine's favourite jewellers than to that of an architect. It is

166 The Palace of Pavlovsk seen from the park, built by Cameron between 1781 and 1796 as a country residence for Paul I. In plan it consists of a rectangular block fronting on to a courtyard which is enclosed by service wings

thus not without reason that her boudoir was known as 'the Empress's snuff-box'.

Strelna was an older palace than Tsarskoe for Michetti spent from 1718 to 1723 building it, and even then the work had to be completed by Tusov. Like all the palaces which Peter built for himself it stood close to the waters of the Gulf of Finland and was in the restrained Baroque style Peter was especially fond of. It was, however, larger in size than Peter's other residences, but the simplicity of its plain façade was broken by a centrally placed archway leading to an inner *cour d'honneur*. For the rest the outer façades of the palace depended for their attraction on the clever spacing of their numerous windows and the balance of their proportions.

Catherine's unfortunate son, the future Paul I, was especially fond of Strelna, but in 1782 Catherine commissioned Cameron to build Pavlovsk as a palace for him whilst he was travelling in Europe with his wife. Paul became interested in the proposal, and eventually grew attached to Pavlovsk as he had been to Strelna. Though habitable by 1784, it was not until the end of the century that the palace was completed, a quarrel between Paul and Cameron having resulted in Brenna and Gonzago being called in to add the rounded wings and to complete some of the interior decorations (*Ill. 166*). In spite of this Pavlovsk remains essentially Cameron's work; it is probably his masterpiece; it also remains the only one of all the Petersburgian palaces to have been built at one stroke, and never to have been subjected to any rebuilding.

Cameron was a middle-aged man by the time he came to Russia. A friend of Cardinal Albani, an admirer of Winkelmann, and an assistant to Clérisseau, to whom he doubtless owed his introduction to Catherine the Great, it is probably in France rather than in England that works by this ardent Jacobite should be sought. Cameron's character was a curious blend of dourness and romanticism. Before starting out for Russia he conceived a largely illusory idea of that country so that he had himself painted wearing pseudo-Russian dress; on reaching his destination he continued to live in this world of make-believe, with the result that his original design for his first commission, the cathedral at Tsarskoe Selo, was in an exotic style which puzzled and displeased the Russians. Though Cameron did not learn a word of Russian during the thirty-odd years which he spent in the country of his adoption, he lost no time in readjusting his views to the taste of its people, developing, after this initial setback, the severe though magnificently ornate and at the same time essentially livable style of Catherine's private apartments at Tsarskoe Selo and of the palace at Pavlovsk (*Ill. 167, 168*). Pavlovsk has been compared to Adam's Kedlestone, but although Cameron must have greatly admired the Adam brothers, since he worked in the style they had made fashionable in England, his buildings are even so more elegant and imaginative, and blend more naturally and harmoniously with their settings. He comes closer to Vanbrugh in his power of associating a building with its surroundings than does any other British architect. It is the unpretentiousness of Pavlovsk which endears the palace to the Russians, an unpretentiousness which is vastly enhanced by the idyllic, dream-like setting which P. Gonzago, working in Russia from 1792 as a follower of Canaletto and Bibiena,

167 The Green Dining Room at the Catherine Palace at Tsarskoe Selo, by Cameron. One of the architect's earliest works for Catherine, it goes far to prove that he derived most of his ideas direct from Rome rather than the Adam brothers, to whom he is often compared

provided for it when he completed the layout of the park and, with the assistance of Simon Shchedrin, decorated the walls of many of its rooms with paintings in perspective.

Gatchina was yet another of the splendid palaces which adorn the outskirts of St Petersburg. Somewhat earlier in date than Pavlovsk, having been built by Rinaldi between 1766 and 1781, it illustrates the transitional phase from the Baroque to the Neo-classic. Its façade verges on starkness, but its rhythm retains the fluidity of the earlier style. The Empress so much admired it that she engaged Rinaldi entirely to rebuild Schädel's Palace of Oranienbaum as well as to construct the Marble Palace in St Petersburg itself (1768–85), which she wished to present to her favourite, Count Orlov.

Elagin, the last of the palaces on the periphery, was an early work of Rossi, having occupied his attention from 1816 to 1826. Grandly conceived, the severity of its style is unrelieved by surface decoration, but it is invested with the grace necessary to enable it to blend with its gentle setting on a hillock, in a charmingly wooded park. It is indeed so skilfully attuned to the landscape that when looking at it, it is difficult to remember that Rossi's great reputation rests on his skill as an urban architect, a designer of streets and squares rather than of country houses.

Nor, with Elizabeth's advent to the throne, was building confined as it had been in Peter's day to St Petersburg. Revel, Mitava, and Kiev were but some of the cities to benefit from the attention of the capital's leading architects; many a country town and rural estate made use of the country's foremost designers. Thomas de Thomon worked in places as far removed as Odessa and Poltava; Cameron built the stately mansions of Baturino and Bakhtcheserai; Quarenghi built the country house of Lialichi near Chernigov in 1794–95 for Count Zavadovski, and the Sheremetievs' Ostankino on what are now the outskirts of Moscow; the Galitzins' mansion of Arkhangelskoe near Moscow, which dated from 1703, was rebuilt after the war of 1812 by Bove. These are but some of the houses which set the standard to which the wealthier landowners aspired. Outside St Petersburg it was, however, in Moscow that the most important work was done. Much of it was produced under the auspices of

168 The Cabinet of Mirrors at the Catherine Palace, Tsarskoe Selo, is another example of Cameron's severe yet extremely luxurious interiors

Bazhenov, Kokorinov, and Kazakov who were all of outstanding ability, and the quality of whose work is testified by the mansion Kazakov built in Moscow for the Batashevs, and which is now a hospital, or by those in St Petersburg which Kokorinov built for the Demidovs and the Shuvalovs. The loss in the fire of 1812 of most of the work for which they had been responsible is irreparable. Over three thousand of the town's nine thousand dwellings and a hundred and thirty of its three hundred churches disappeared in the flames. On Napoleon's withdrawal from the town a building commission was set up under the chairmanship of Kokorinov to deal with the task of rebuilding the ruined town; the commission entrusted many of the most important undertakings, such as the university building (1817–20) and the Razumovski Palace to the Italian architect Domenico Gilliardi, but it was the numerous houses which the Russian architects working for private patrons built in a diversity of styles that produced the picturesque effects which led many a late-nineteenth-century visitor to Russia to lose his heart to Moscow, preferring its wayward beauty to the ordered loveliness of St Petersburg.

Yet St Petersburg was as Russian a town as Moscow, for not only had the foreigners who were generally the ones to be selected for the most important undertakings to take the taste of their Russian patrons into full account, but they had too to work with Russian assistants. It was from the latter that they learnt to work on the grand scale which is characteristic of Russia; from them that they acquired the art of using windows as a means not only of lighting the interiors, but also of decorating the façades of their buildings; it was also due to the Russian affection for the column—an affection which resulted in the column usurping in the eighteenth and nineteenth centuries the place which the dome had held in the Early Christian period— that columns became an integral feature of Russian architecture. Their presence in all building of quality endowed the work even of foreigners with an essentially Russian appearance, just as the Russian delight in a kind of sumptuous 'cosiness' resulted in even the most formal suite of apartments acquiring a livable quality which is rarely to be found in equivalent buildings in Western Europe.

Sculpture and the Minor Arts

Much of the fascination which imperial Russia exercised over foreign visitors was due to the radiance of the Russian interior. Rastrelli had set a new standard at Peterhof, the Winter Palace at St Petersburg, and the Catherine Palace at Tsarskoe Selo which Cameron had maintained at Pavlovsk. The note struck by the wall-decorations in the palaces and country houses was sustained in them by the beauty of the furniture (*Ill. 169*), much of which was specifically made for the rooms in which it stood to the design of a great architect. Russian carpenters had always excelled at making beds, chairs, tables, cupboards, and cabinets of various types, and the country cottage had seldom lacked charm. The architects whom the Russian sovereigns and notables employed as their builders could thus indulge their every fancy when designing furnishings and fittings, being able to enhance them not only with inlay, gilding, and ormolu, but with the marbles and semi-precious stones in which Siberia is so rich (*Ill. 170*). In remoter districts many a serf proved as capable as the town cabinet-maker of carrying out the wishes of his westernized masters, though the imaginative quality which had inspired many peasant carvers in the Muscovite period appeared to decline.

It is curious that even when the carver's skill was at its height the Russian showed little wish for objects worked in the round, whether in wood, stone, or some precious material. Ivan III had attempted to create a demand in Moscow for sculptured figures by commissioning from Vasili Ermolin (died 1485), a builder who ran a stone-carver's workshop, two figures with which to decorate the Kremlin's Frolov Gate, which was soon after replaced by the Redeemer's Gate. Part of one of them survives (*Ill. 171*); it consists of the head and shoulders of what was once an equestrian statue of St George shown in the act of killing the dragon. This fragment represents Russia's earliest known figural sculpture in the round, though animal figures in the

169 A late-eighteenth-century table in gilt wood elaborately carved and fitted
with a malachite top

round had been produced in the pre-Mongol invasion period in the
Principality of Vladimir-Suzdal. However, Ermolin's fragment is too
accomplished a work not to have had forerunners; but none of these
survives. Nor does this sculpture, for all its grace, appear to have
inspired any contemporary artists to produce work in the same vein.
Only in the eighteenth century, under the impact of one of Europe's
great artists, Carlo Bartolommeo Rastrelli (1675–1744), the father of
Elizabeth's brilliant architect, did the Russians become conscious of
the beauty and scope of sculpture in the round.

Rastrelli the elder came to Russia in 1716, intending to stay for
three years only, yet he remained there till his death, endowing his
adopted country with a well-nigh unrivalled series of portrait busts

170 An urn in malachite and ormolu, *c.* 1815. The rich deposits of marble and semi-precious stones which were being exploited in Siberia led to a demand for urns and vessels made in these materials and mounted in elaborately ornamented bronze fittings

(*Ill. 172*), plaques, and medals. His son inherited his father's appreciation of sculpture, using full-length figures to adorn the roof-tops of his buildings, and an immense variety of work in high relief to embellish his long façades. The beauty revealed by sculpture of this type and quality led to the creation at the Academy of Fine Arts of a school of sculpture. The Frenchman Nicolas-François Gillet (1709–91) became its first Director, and under his guidance the Russians learnt the technique of this difficult medium. Gillet's pupils included some of the best sculptors Russia has known, men such as Gordeev, Shchedrin, Kozlovski, and Martos, though none of these was ever to equal the son of a White Sea fisherman, the largely self-taught Fedot Shubin.

171 A fragment from an equestrian statue of St George by Ermolin, *c.* 1480. This is the earliest major work in the round known to us. With a companion piece, which disappeared long ago, it formed part of the decorations of the Frolov Gate in Moscow's Kremlin

F. F. Shchedrin (1751–1825) followed Gillet's example and produced idealized figures of Hellenistic form imbued with the sentimentality which was the inevitable adjunct of the Romantic Age; however, his Greek-like goddesses were extremely popular among his contemporaries, whilst the two statues with which he adorned the main entrance to Zakharov's Admiralty are truly fine. Nevertheless, today Gordeev (1744–1810) appears the more interesting artist, and perhaps the more genuinely inspired of the two; he was the more clearly conscious of the possibilities inherent in sculpture and his *Prometheus* is an adventurous and well-conceived work. Even so, it is Fedot Shubin (1740–1805) who still today represents the best in Russian sculpture. Shubin was a realist, but his concern with everyday life was tempered in him by Gillet, who taught him the value of elegance. The creative period of Shubin's life as a professional artist embraces only sixteen years, yet in that short span he was able to produce a series of portrait busts of outstanding quality (*Ill. 175*). Truthfulness prevails in them, but it is

172 Bronze bust of Peter the Great, by Rastrelli the elder, 1724. The Tsar's contemporaries considered the bust a striking likeness; indeed its vitality is just as much at variance with the fitted traditional elegance of eighteenth-century drapery as was the Tsar's personality with the refinements of Western life. The bust is a magnificent portrait

allied to grace, so that each bust appears as a perceptive and admirably executed portrait which, as in the case of Levitski's paintings, is enhanced by all the brilliant accessories then fashionable.

Shubin left no one of a like quality to follow in his steps, but the latter half of the eighteenth century was enriched by the equestrian statue of Peter the Great which stands in the Senate Square in Leningrad, mounted on a superb block of granite. The statue is one of the world's great sculptures, the work of the Frenchman Falconet, who spent from 1766 to 1768 in St Petersburg sculpting the horse and the Sovereign's body, letting his pupil, Marthe Callot, copy the face from masks of Peter taken both in his lifetime and his death.

While Shubin was creating his vivid portrait busts and Falconet his masterpiece, another of Gillet's pupils, M. I. Kozlovski (1753–c. 1802), was beginning to attract attention. After spending some years in Rome, Kozlovski had returned to St Petersburg to win fame for himself by heroic studies executed in the pseudo-Classical style which Gillet and Shchedrin had popularized. Kozlovski worked

173 (*left*) Mortuary monument to Princess Gagarina, by Martos. The statue stands above her grave in the Lazarus cemetery at Leningrad

174 (*right*) Bronze monument to General Suvorov by Kozlovski. The figure and elderly appearance of the General did not lend themselves to treatment in the fashionable Classical style and the sculptor was therefore forced to disguise them by presenting Suvorov in the form of Mars. It is a tribute to his skill that he avoided making his sitter appear ridiculous

both in the round and in low relief; the slabs with which he decorated the façade of the Marble Palace are of a high standard, but his finest work was the powerful figure of *Samson* which he made for the main cascade of Peterhof in 1800–02—a work the disappearance of which in the course of the last war represents a major loss. In it

194

175 Marble bust of Count A. G. Orlovski, by Fedot Shubin, 1771. Notwithstanding the conventional manner of presentation the bust is a superb likeness, a profound psychological document, and a most accomplished piece of sculpture

Kozlovski proved that he was capable of creating as dynamic and spirited a figure as Gordeev's *Prometheus*. His monument to Suvorov (*Ill. 174*) is both energetic and dignified and has stood the test of time. The last sculptor in the line of Gillet's pupils was Martos (1754–1835), who himself became a teacher at the Academy, where he in his turn formed a large number of most competent followers. In his day Martos enjoyed immense popularity, being especially admired for his funerary monuments. The majority of these are in the Hellenistic style favoured by Gillet, but as in the case of Princess Gagarina's monument (*Ill. 173*) Martos was able to invest his commemorative figures with a marked nobility. M. I. Pimenov (1784–

1833), a pupil of Kozlovski, was also much sought after for funerary monuments. He was more forthright in his approach, but today he appears at his best in his Classical compositions. His most ambitious bronze, one of Hercules, is an accomplished work. Pimenov's contemporary B. Demut-Malinovski (1779–1846) was no less skilled but, like many painters of his day, he became deeply concerned in political issues, and his Slavophile sympathies led him to turn to native subjects for inspiration; illogically, he rendered them in a Hellenistic style which ill suits them so that he is to be seen at his best in his portrait busts. Another contemporary, P. K. Klodt (1805–67), became Russia's first animal sculptor; he was particularly fond of modelling horses, and the equestrian group on the Anichkov Bridge in Leningrad is one of his best works (*Ill. 176*); his monument to Kryllov, the eminent fabulist, in the Summer Gardens is as much loved by the children of Leningrad as is the statue of Peter Pan in Kensington Gardens by Londoners.

The Summer Gardens are the oldest in Leningrad for their layout had been begun even before the start of Peter's Summer Palace. They were embellished at an early date by the construction of a vast pavilion, the first, and perhaps most important work of Zemtzov. Its success was such that pavilions, temples, and hermitages came very much into vogue. Those Rastrelli designed for the park at Tsarskoe Selo were among the most imaginative, for they included such architectural gems as the Hermitage, which was fitted out with a dining-table which could be automatically lowered to the kitchen, and thus made the presence of servants in the dining-room unnecessary, as well as the exquisite pavilion of Mon Bijou, a fascinating grotto and an enchanting toboggan hill. The park at Pavlovsk was particularly delightful; its poetic atmosphere was sustained by a series of pavilions, towers, and bridges which, though built in different styles with the result that each was concealed from the sight of the others, yet formed a chain which linked each to its neighbour as they radiated from the palace. Leblond and Rastrelli had been the first to work in the Chinese style in Russia, resorting to it in the parks surrounding their palaces for the aviaries and toboggan hills with which they set out to enliven the melancholy Petersburgian landscape. Then the

176 One of four bronze equestrian groups which adorn the Anichkov Bridge at Leningrad, by Baron P. K. Klodt, 1839. They form impressive embellishments to one of Europe's loveliest cities

English Garden drew the attention of the Russians so that English glades soon came to conceal exotic hermitages and severe pavilions, whilst adjacent alleys of French origin continued to serve as a setting for Italian statues and jets of water rising from intricately devised fountains. But the Russian park with its delicate acacias and unruly lilacs soon smoothed the contours of both, veiling them in a wholly Russian informality.

Much use continued to be made throughout westernized Russia of wrought and cast iron. More sophisticated and graceful designs were evolved in St Petersburg than elsewhere for balcony rails and other street fittings, and at the same time both the range and the number of metal objects produced for use in the home increased greatly. Some of the earlier work may well have been done by craftsmen who had received their initial training in the workshops of the Palace

197

177 Two extremely fine enamelled plaques showing respectively the Archangel
Gabriel and the Archangel Michael. Muscovite work of between 1680 and 1700 of
excellent design and execution

of Arms at Moscow, but who were diverted to the munitions factory
which Peter the Great had established at Tula in 1711, when he closed
down the Palace of Arms workshops. When the need for munitions
had been met the men were employed on other work; this included
the production of steel furniture, mantelpieces, and urns of splendid
design and extremely delicate workmanship (*Ill. 178, 179*).

The Russians have always taken a great delight in fine jewellery
and metalwork. It was a taste which both Elizabeth I and Catherine
the Great shared so that, under their rule, jewellery and metalwork
experienced a remarkable revival. The demand for enamels, which
had grown up in Moscow in the sixteenth century (*Ill. 177*), persisted
in St Petersburg, many lovely objects being produced in a great
range of delicate colours. However, Catherine was not herself fond
of bright colours, and for her use a series of extremely beautiful

178 Chair in cut steel made at the Tula Foundry; late eighteenth century. Furniture of this type is extremely rare, the cut steel having been chiefly used for the making of small ornaments, such as those placed on the mantelpiece shown below

179 This cut-steel mantelpiece complete with fender and fire-irons is probably unique. Oman's suggestion that it was sent by Princess Dashkova in 1802 as a gift for Martha Wilmot is almost certainly correct. Of the ornaments adorning it the candlesticks disappeared during the last war

199

180 A Turkish coffee set consisting of a tray and six cups in opaque white enamel on copper adorned with silver plaques. Period of Catherine the Great. The floral decorations on the cups resemble some of the sculptured flowers on the façade of the thirteenth-century Cathedral of St George at Yuriev-Polski. Made in Velikij Ustuig

opaque white or deep blue enamelled objects decorated with delicate bronze motifs were especially made (*Ill. 180*). The jewellery produced at this time was also of outstanding delicacy and beauty, but it is among the snuff-boxes (*Ill. 182, 183, 187*), for which French influence had created a demand, that the greatest artistry is perhaps to be found. The skill and ingenuity devoted to the production of these boxes, whether they were made of gold, silver, semi-precious stones, niello, or enamel, is truly astonishing. Many of them are works of art of the highest quality. The delight taken in fine metalwork was such that Catherine could not resist on occasion herself designing some of the pieces she wished to have made as presentation gifts (*Ill. 181*). Articles of personal adornment (*Ill. 186*), tableware, church vessels, swords of honour, and amusing trifles were prized throughout the country for their workmanship. Indeed, the tradition of fine jewellery and metalwork endured till the Revolution.

181 A gold embossed chalice, St Petersburg, 1791. Designed by Catherine the Great as a presentation gift to the Monastery of St Alexander in St Petersburg, in memory of Prince Potyemkin

182 (*below*) Gold and enamel *bonbonnière* signed: 'Ador, St Petersburg'. Ador was one of the great goldsmiths of his day and this box is a good example of his work

183 (*above*) A gold and enamel box bearing a portrait in enamel of a man who has been tentatively identified either as Count Ivan Chernyshaev or as Count Vladimir Orlov. Hallmarked St Petersburg, 1773

184 (*right*) An engraved and gilt glass with cover bearing the monogram of Elizabeth I and the imperial eagle in gold, the characteristic form of decoration for glass made for members of the royal family

187 (*far right*) Gold snuff-box studded with diamonds signed by Ador, adorned with six enamel plaques by Kaestern. This is assuredly Ador's masterpiece. Catherine commissioned the box as a gift for Count Gregory Orlov who helped her to assume power. The enamels cover the events which brought Catherine to the throne in 1764. The top panel shows her receiving the homage of her people on being proclaimed Empress; that below shows her on the balcony of the unfinished Winter Palace holding the future Paul I in her arms

185 Miniature of Catherine the Great in a frame made of two shades of gold. Though Rokotov is not known to have painted any miniatures, the style of this portrait is so close to his that it has been suggested that it may well be by his hand. The frame bears the St Petersburg hallmark and the date 1784

186 (*below*) Watch and *chatelaine pavé* in diamonds bearing the monogram of Catherine the Great in rubies. The inside of the watch is inscribed in script: 'D. T. Muscard, St Petersburg'. A gift from Catherine to her granddaughter, who married the Prince of Saxe-Weiman

Fabergé was the last in a long line of artists to devote themselves to fashioning objects of the highest artistry. The needs of the less sophisticated and prosperous sections of the community were catered for by the jewellers of Tula, Vladimir, and the Caucasian area, many of whom were craftsmen of quite outstanding ability.

Though glass factories had existed in Kiev and Kostroma in Early Christian times they closed down at the time of the Mongol occupation, and the industry was not re-established until 1637 when a Swede called Elias Koet set up a factory at Mozhaisk. In 1668 another was founded at Izmailovo near Moscow, whilst the closing decades of the century saw the establishment of one within Moscow's Kremlin enclosure. An even larger one was in production at Yamburg by 1717, by which time Peter had also founded the Imperial Factory on the Sparrow Hills outside Moscow. It was soon after amalgamated with the Yamburg Factory, and both were transferred to St Petersburg by the middle of the eighteenth century when a school and experimental workshops were added to them (*Ill. 184, 189*). It was in these that the coloured glass and mosaic pictures were made in the latter quarter of the century. By that time the establishment had come to be regarded as the best of its kind and the various glass factories which came into being in the course of the nineteenth century modelled themselves on it.

The manufacture of china took longer to establish. The method of its production remained unknown throughout the whole of the medieval period. Peter was the first to try to master it. In 1708 he employed a foreigner called Eggerbank to establish a factory in St Petersburg, but although the man came to Russia as arranged nothing is known about his activities there. Elizabeth was equally anxious to establish a porcelain factory in the capital and, on coming to the throne, she engaged Konrad Hunger of Stockholm to found one, but she also attached a Russian called Vinogradov to act both as his pupil and his supervisor. Not content with this, she instructed an officer called Lebratovski to lead a caravan to China to discover the secret there. Lebratovski engaged an Armenian silversmith called Andrei Kursin to accompany him. When the two men eventually reached their destination they set out to persuade a Chinese potter to show them his recipe book and to demonstrate his skill by a bribe of a thousand roubles. Even so, they failed to master the essentials of the craft, and when they returned to St Petersburg neither proved capable of making china; by this time too Hunger had proved to be no better than a charlatan. At his dismissal in 1748, Vinogradov, who as a science scholar of the Academy had been sent abroad in 1730 to study chemistry and physics, was appointed to replace Hunger. By trial and error it was he who eventually managed to produce china of good quality, thus making the establishment of the Imperial Porcelain Factory possible (*Ill. 188, 190, 195, 196*). By 1750 Vinogradov was taking orders for tableware; within another year he was producing excellent snuff-boxes, and by 1752 he was turning out the figurines for which the factory was to become famous. Only some twenty of these early pieces survive; all are at the Hermitage Museum. They include figurines of blackamoors, some chess pawns, and several allegorical pieces. Catherine expanded the factory and encouraged the production of armorial porcelain and of a larger range of figurines. The latter continued to be made in ever-growing numbers under Paul I, a series of street sellers and regional costumes being added. The range of tableware was also greatly widened, and at the same time experiments were started in the making of biscuitware. Under Alexander I views of palaces and towns became very popular, but Nicholas I encouraged the introduction of regimental uniforms and military subjects. By this time porcelain factories had come into existence in a number of provincial towns, Vyatka being noted for its comic figurines and Okhta for its satirical ones of rich and pompous Petersburgians. Among the more important ceramic factories established outside the capital was that which the Englishman Francis Gardner founded in 1750 in a village on the outskirts of Moscow (*Ill. 191, 192, 197*); he produced a good deal of the china used in the royal dining-rooms; his factory was called after him and remained in being under his descendants till 1891 when it was bought by the Kusnetzov porcelain works. The equally famous Popov Factory was started near Moscow in 1811, the Poskochin, Kozlov, Batemin, and Sofronov factories being the best known among the numerous factories of more recent date.

188 (*above left*) One of a pair of porcelain vases with ormolu handles and mounts, made at the Imperial Porcelain Factory. The vase is marked with the cipher of Catherine II

189 (*above right*) One of a pair of girandoles made in St Petersburg between 1790 and 1800

190 (*left*) A plate from a service made for Elizabeth I in the Imperial Porcelain Factory. It is marked on the back with an eagle in black

191 (*above*) A splendid pair of large vases from the Baktiny Factory decorated with views of St Petersburg; early nineteenth century

192 (*right*) A plate from the large service now at Pavlovsk made partly at the Imperial Porcelain Factory and partly at Gardner's factory to celebrate the marriage of Paul I to Marie. The plate bears their interlocked initials as its central design. It carries the mark of the Imperial Porcelain Factory

193 A carved block for stamping textiles, *c.* 1800. There is a strong element of folk art in the design of the birds and animals

From the twelfth century onwards linen was woven in Russia, when some of that which was intended for making into vestments, tent hangings, or Gospel covers was decorated with stamped designs. The wooden stamps (*Ill. 193*) which were used for the purpose were very elaborately carved and were then dipped in vegetable dyes which had been mixed by icon painters who alone at the time knew the art of making colours. In the post-Mongol period much of the textile industry was concentrated round Yaroslavl and Kostroma, where the workers gradually took over from the icon painters the task of mixing the dyes; later factories with large outputs, often using poor-quality dyes, sprang up at Vyatka, Vologda, and Olonetz.

194 A Bessarabian *kilim* of mid-nineteenth-century date. This is typical of the style which was popular at the time. Large rose heads shown against foliage are especially characteristic. Under the impact of Turkish influence, tulips were a favourite motif, though they were sometimes replaced by different flowers. The colours in this example are deep rose, green, and off-white on a black ground

195 Lustre tea service decorated with medallions containing views of St Petersburg and one of Gatchina. Made in the Imperial Porcelain Factory under Alexander I and marked in blue, *c.* 1820

196 A plate decorated with a military scene of the type specially admired by Nicholas I, described on the back as 'Officier superieur et subalterne du Regt de la Garde à Cheval'; the plate bears the cypher of Nicholas I and the mark of the Imperial Porcelain Factory

197 A tea service by Gardner dating from the 1820s; it is decorated with figures and scenes painted in the style of the factory's figurines as well as with the arms of Prince Kassatkin-Rostovski

198 An early-nineteenth-century brocade bearing the type of floral design which was especially popular at the time

By that time, however, Peter's unsuccessful attempts to introduce the manufacture of high-quality fabrics had been realized by Elizabeth, with the result that, from at any rate the second half of the eighteenth century, brocades (*Ill. 198*) and silks of such high quality were being produced that it is sometimes difficult to distinguish them from French materials. Indeed, the best pieces may well have been made by foreign technicians working in Russia or by Russians working under foreign supervision. Garlands often figure prominently in the designs of these fabrics, though posies of roses or single flowers set against a gold or silver ground are scarcely less characteristic. Sage green as well as the peculiarly Russian tones of pink and yellow, and also rather a Victorian shade of purple remained extremely popular till late in the nineteenth century.

Though the Russians had from a very early date made widespread use of carpets first in their tents, then in their mud huts, and later still in their wooden houses, they found it easier to obtain the rugs they wanted by acquiring them from their Eastern neighbours rather than making them for themselves. Indeed, although Peter the Great had established a tapestry-weaving factory in 1717 with the aid of French technicians, all of whom had been replaced by Russians by the middle of the eighteenth century, no attempt was made in Western Russia to produce carpets till the nineteenth century. Then Kursk and Voronezh became the centres for the making of *kilims* which were similar to those which had been produced from a rather earlier date in the Ukraine, Moldavia, and Bessarabia under the influence of Aubusson carpets. The majority of the Russian *kilims* have a dark ground with brightly coloured flowers worked on them (*Ill. 194*). The finer examples are often of considerable size and of such high quality that they attain to true artistic merit. Rugs of this type continued to be made for several decades after the closing down in 1859 of the tapestry factory which Peter had founded; then they too went out of production, machine-made carpets or rugs imported from the East again sufficing to satisfy the existing demand.

Painters had greater difficulty in adjusting themselves to Western convention than had the architects and the craftsmen responsible for the flowering of the minor arts. Under pressure from Peter artists were expected to bridge in one Herculean stride the gap dividing the wholly religious, stylized art of the icon painter from the naturalistic, immeasurably wider field of Western art. That the change was rapidly effected was largely due to the high standard set by the more eminent foreigners who had come to work in Russia, men such as Le Lorrain, Lagrenée, and Tocqué to name but these; but the measures taken by Peter to produce Russian artists by founding a school of drawing at the St Petersburg Printing House and by sending more 'fledglings' to study abroad were equally important.

Even so, for many decades to come Russian artists were to feel more at ease in portraiture than in other types of painting. Portraiture had, as we have seen, begun to fascinate Moscow's icon painters as early as the first part of the seventeenth century. The humanistic attitude to life which was an essential part of the Russian make-up may well have rendered painters better suited to this type of art than to any other; their centuries-old experience in depicting men's sentiments and aspirations also doubtless helped to endow them with a certain amount of psychological insight. As a result some professional artists, as distinct from the domestic painters, who were often self-taught serfs, were in the process of adapting themselves to the new formulas even before these were forced upon them. This is evident from a series of portraits of dwarfs painted in about 1690 by Adolski (*Ill. 199*); though still revealing links with religious mural painting in their rather flatly laid on colours, they are closer to Western art than to the iconic portraits produced several decades earlier; in their psychological content no less than in their naturalism they quite definitely belong to the new age.

199 Portrait of Peter I's fool Yakov Turgenev, by Adolski. Painted at the end of the seventeenth century it was far in advance of its time, and is one of the earliest examples of true portraiture

The age of Peter the Great was proclaimed in painting by a group of the Tsar's fledglings, which included four artists of distinction: Ivan Nikitin (1688–1741), Andrei Matveev (1701–39), Alexis Antropov (1716–95), and Ivan Argunov (1727–1803) (*Ill. 201*). All four were of humble birth, and all four mastered the new idiom sufficiently well to become competent portraitists. Their merit lay in their ability to produce lucid compositions, in their quite profound understanding of character and, above all, in their deep sincerity and high degree of integrity—qualities which they were to hand down to following generations of artists. None of the four was, however, altogether at ease in the new idiom and none was able to produce works of truly high pictorial quality, though Antropov could paint drapery skilfully and render the texture of fine fabrics (*Ill. 202*). He was commissioned to paint a number of royal portraits, but the icons which he produced in his closing years for the Cathedral of St Andrew at Kiev, which Rastrelli had designed, were of greater interest than most of his portraits.

200 Portrait of Princess Dashkova, born Vorontzov (1743–1810), by Levitski, 1784. The Princess played no small part in helping to bring Catherine the Great to the throne. She was very fond of Martha Wilmot and bequeathed this portrait to her in her will

For more accomplished and sophisticated work it is necessary to look to the next generation of painters, to men such as Rokotov, Borovikovski, and, above all, to the somewhat earlier Levitski, for it is the latter who stands out as the great figure in Russian eighteenth-century painting. Feodor Rokotov's life covered the longest span, extending from 1735 to 1808. As upright and sincere an artist as his four predecessors his portrait of Peter III and of the future Paul I, painted when the latter was only seven years old, show great discernment as well as considerable moral courage, since the artist made no attempt to gloss over the less attractive characteristics of his royal patrons (*Ill. 203*). Borovikovski and Levitski both display a like integrity with far more technical proficiency. Both were born in the Ukraine at a time when the region was in regular touch with the Western world, and this contact with Europe may have helped the artists rapidly to adjust themselves to the Western style of painting. Though by profession a soldier, Vladimir Borovikovski (1757–1825) was able whilst still a young man to attend some lessons given by the slightly older Levitski, and although he never succeeded, nor indeed did he ever attempt, to probe very deeply into the technical problems of his calling, he was nevertheless able to paint well (*Ill. 204*). Catherine admired his attractive style and was ready to pose for him. His picture showing her walking her dog in the park at Tsarskoe Selo is surely one of the most unaffected portraits of a sovereign ever to have been painted; in its informality it set a precedent which was followed by other painters of royalty, notably, a century later, by Serov in his fine portrait of Nicholas II (*Ill. 222*). Borovikovski's portrait of Catherine is an excellent as well as an interesting painting, though it is not as experimental a work as some of his other pictures.

It is unfortunate that Catherine never sat for Dmitri Levitski (1735–1822), who can be termed the Gainsborough of Russian art. Admirably taught, first by his father, a noted if somewhat dry engraver, then by Antropov, who had by that time established a school which set out to provide a freer training than that offered by the Academy, Levitski mastered all the technical problems of his calling in his early life and became an experienced professional. He

201 (*left*) This Portrait of a Peasant girl, by Argunov, 1784, is the first painting of a peasant by the hand of an artist fully trained in the Western style of painting

202 (*right*) Portrait of the Ataman Krasnoshchekhov, by Antropov, 1761; an extremely competent painting

chose to produce portraits painted in the grand manner, yet none of these is in any sense an academic picture; each is imbued with vitality, and the majority stand out both as works of art and as fascinating records of the personality and idiosyncracies of the great personages of his day (*Ill. 200*). This is especially true of the portraits which Levitski produced before old age had dimmed his perception and darkened his palette.

It was Catherine I who, in 1727, raised Peter's school of drawing to a department of art incorporated in the Academy of Sciences, but it was Catherine the Great who then elevated it in 1767 to the status of an independent Academy of Fine Arts. Under Peter and

203 Portrait of Mrs V. N. Surovtseva, by Rokotov, 1780; which again serves to show that artists of this period set more store on achieving a physical and psychological likeness than in creating elegant effects

Catherine I the teaching in the earlier foundations had aimed at creating artists, but under Catherine II the purpose of the Academy's course seems to have consisted in evolving an official form of art rather than in developing the individuality of its students. From the start the students in each of the imperial schools had received an excellent technical grounding, but it was not till the end of the century that this training began to take full effect. Then artists such as Feodor Bruni (1800–1875) and Karl Brüllov (1799–1852) appeared, to display the skill and versatility which can only be attained through full mastery over the chosen medium, but by that time they, and more particularly Bruni, had also become deeply imbued with the Academy's circumscribed, dogmatic outlook. As a result he combined a stiff, academic classicism of style with the mystical approach of the Nazarene painters, and for all the skill with which he evolved his compositions, today his work seems lifeless and uninspired.

204 Portrait of Mrs Skobeeva, by Borovikovski. Though showing more interest in composition than does the work of Rokotov the artist displays a similar striving for truth

Karl Brüllov was equally proficient and possessed in addition a more genuinely artistic temperament. It was he who at this period epitomized all that was best in the Academy's training (*Ill. 206*). His lively mind, eclectic interests, and warm enthusiasms enabled him to respond spontaneously and often vividly to new experiences, to approach each theme with a fresh eye, and to show himself ready to experiment and wrestle with technical difficulties. Today some of his canvases, like his famous *Last Day of Pompeii*, tend to seem uninteresting; others, like his *Italian Noon*, to appear over-sentimental. But reactions such as these are as much the result of fashion as are the themes he chose for these pictures. Brüllov was Russia's first all-round artist, and because of this he will always remain important; even today, when tastes are dominated by the appeal of a very different style, the pictorial qualities in many of his pictures, and especially in his portraits, are clearly evident.

205 *Dancing Bacchante*, engraving, identified by Sir Anthony Blunt as by Poussin, copied by Bazhenov, 1784. Though better known as an architect Bazhenov was also an artist of considerable quality. Indeed in Paris, where he studied for two years, he would have been awarded the Prix de Rome had he not been a foreigner. In Russia his delicate humour and fine draughtmanship tended to pass unnoticed and few of his pictures have survived

The academic outlook was deeply rooted in Brüllov yet, like so many of his contemporaries, he too often responded to the canons of taste created by the Romantic movement, though his training saved him from succumbing to excessive sentimentality as did many of his contemporaries. Indeed, only two painters, both of them the sons of serfs, were true Romantics who succeeded in imbuing their works with the Byronic spirit without ever turning it into a formula. The greatest of the two was Orest Kiprenski (1782–1836). His genius carried him to the Academy and his work is as a result very accomplished, but it is owing to his innate artistic abilities that it is also almost always interesting. Passionate in his approach and endowed with a better sense of colour than most of his contemporaries, his portraits are not only valuable records of the period, but often also true works of art (*Ill. 207*). Vasili Tropinin (1776–1857) was another

206 *The Rider*, by Brüllov, 1832, shows the artist at his best, revealing his technical mastery, his fine sense of composition, and his feeling for elegance and grace. The Romantic spirit which pervades the painting enhances its appeal for it is devoid of the sentimentality which mars so many paintings of this period

Romantic to receive his training at the Academy, but he remained throughout his life a less well-educated man than Kiprenski. This limitation is reflected in his paintings (*Ill. 208*) which, though profoundly sincere, and as such important to the historian, have not the same aesthetic value as Kiprenski's works.

The foundations of historical and landscape painting were also laid in the eighteenth century for Russia's first historical picture, a reconstruction of the Battle of Kulikovo, is now generally ascribed to Nikitin. However, it was not until Catherine the Great's newly established Academy of Fine Arts had proclaimed that 'art must aim at revealing virtue, at immortalizing the deeds of the great men who deserve the nation's gratitude, and at encouraging the heart and mind to emulate them' that historical painting became part of the Academy's curriculum. Unfortunately the themes which were set in

207 Self-portrait, by Kiprenski. Though treated in the Romantic manner the artist's profound integrity has resulted in the exclusion of all artificiality and sentimentality

the classes were invariably drawn from mythological or Classical sources, and were therefore devoid of any sense of actuality. The students were not moved by them and were apt, therefore, to treat the subjects in a purely illustrative way, without striving to arouse in others the emotions they themselves did not feel, refraining even from creating interesting colour effects. Indeed, it is impossible not to wonder what had become of the Russians' innate sense of colour

208 Portrait of K. G. Ravich, by Tropinin, 1825, is a confident, forceful, and pleasing painting

for, with the country's westernization, it disappeared for almost two centuries from the works of the major artists, though it continued to flourish among the people as a whole. Indeed, with the introduction in the 1820s of a cheap lithographic process, the presses working for the masses produced a great many prints, the majority of which were delightfully coloured. These versions of the English 'penny plain, twopence coloured' sheets are known as *lubki* in Russian (singular

ТРУДОЛЮБИВЫЙ МЕДВѢДЬ

Увидя что мужикъ трудится надъ дугами
Исъ прибылью большой сбываетъ онъ ихъ съ рукъ
А дуги гнуть съ терпѣньемъ и не вдругъ
Медвѣдь задумалъ жить такими же трудами
Вдругъ полосу пошолъ игрескъ истуку
Что слышно заверсту медведя все проказы
Орешнику березнику и вязы
Мой мишка погубилъ несчетное число
А мишъ недается такое ремесло

Идетъ нашъ мишка къ мужику проситъ совѣта
Иговоритъ ему что запрядчина эта
Деревьевъ много я ломать могу
А не согнулъ какъ ты ни одного въ дугу
Скажи мой кумъ любезный и сосѣдъ
Въ чемъ главное твое умѣнье
А нѣтомъ сказалъ мужикъ въ отвѣтъ
Бываетъ много и трудовъ данетъ долготерпѣнья

209 An undated *lubok* drawn in the style of religious prints of the eighteenth century; it illustrates Kryllov's fable *The Industrious Bear*. The scene is set in a forest clearing and shows a peasant carrying part of his horse's harness whilst the bear smashes a sapling

form: *lubok*) (*Ill. 209*). Many reflect the same spirit as that which had in medieval times inspired the naturalistic capital letters of Novgorodian manuscripts, but the *lubok* owed its origin to Peter the Great's efforts to make printed books widely available by encouraging the use of engravings. The printing industry established itself primarily at Vladimir whence it disseminated among the people cheap engravings which had often been designed by peasant artists. Many were religious in character, many were legendary or allegorical, some were humorous, and some acidly satirical and political in content. Thus, at Peter's death, a series was produced on the theme of 'when the cat's away the mice will play' in order to express the peasant's relief at the death of the Sovereign who had tightened the bonds of their serfdom. In the nineteenth century colour brought vitality and beauty to these gay and spirited illustrations, many of which are spiced with the peasant's malicious powers of observation.

210 A study for the figure of the Imbecile by Surikov for his historical painting *The Boyarina Morozova*, 1887. In the final version the figure is shown bearded, and looking older and less inspired

Historical painting, that is painting which recreates the mood and tensions of a specific period, did not come into being till Surikov (1848–1916) turned to Russia's past for the subjects of his pictures. Although a realist painter, he never became a narrative one; he was far too fascinated by people to do so (*Ill. 210*), averring that he could not express the past in a single personage, however important, but

211 View of the St Peter and St Paul Fortress, St Petersburg, with the Palace Quay in the distance, by Alekseev, 1799. For all its many qualities and late date the picture is more in the nature of a topographical record than a true landscape

had to present events against a background of ordinary people. Like Tolstoy's, his canvas was a vast one; he was also able to make it a vivid one, for he was one of the very few artists of the period to use a colourful palette. In addition, Surikov possessed an instinctive understanding of nature, and the glimpses of landscape in the backgrounds of his pictures acted as a stimulus, inspiring artists such as A. Kuinzhi (1842–1910), I. Ayvazovski (1817–1900), and I. Levitan (1861–1900) to create a school of landscape and marine painting.

Their landscapes were the outcome of many decades of experiment. Topographical pictures had, it is true, been produced in St Petersburg from the latter part of the eighteenth century when artists such as Simon Shchedrin (1745–1804), the serf-born Andrei Voronykhin (1760–1814), who is better known for his architectural

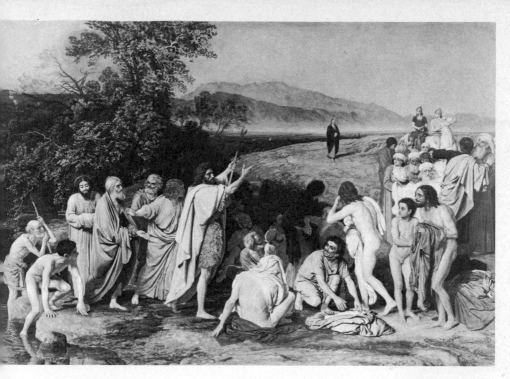

212 *Christ before the People*, by A. A. Ivanov, 1833–55. The artist was so anxious to produce a religious painting which would arouse as much admiration as Brüllov's secular picture *The Last Day of Pompeii* that he devoted twenty years to research and preliminary sketches before producing his major work; yet it is far from being his masterpiece

work, above all Feodor Alekseev (1753–1824), and Feodor Matveev (1758–1826) had all created paintings of consequence. But however attractive as views and important as topographical documents (*Ill. 211*), these works are as far removed from true landscape as the iconic portraits are from true portraiture. Silvester Shchedrin (1791–1830) was thus the first to produce evocative views; indeed, but for his premature death he might well have bridged the final gap, for his pictures of Italy, some of which represent the first Russian attempts to paint the sea, are brilliantly coloured and well composed, and only a touch of imaginative tension is needed to transform them into great works of art.

Alexander Ivanov (1806–58) is the outstanding artist of this period. Versatile and inspired, he received his early training from his father

Andrei as well as from other members of the Academy's staff. He became technically proficient early in his life, but it was only after spending some years in Italy that he was able to express his own individuality in his paintings. Devout as well as romantic by temperament, he devoted much of his time to religious subjects (*Ill. 212*), revealing in their compositions a visionary imagery which is not unlike Blake's. Ivanov also painted some fine Italian landscapes, as well as some of the loveliest, and also the earliest nudes in Russian painting; in addition, he was one of the first artists to take an interest in character painting.

Ivanov's skill in this field was probably developed in the course of his studies in the 'class of domestic exercises', which had been founded at the Academy in the mid eighteenth century with the aim of producing a school of genre painters. The first Russian to benefit from it was Alexei Venetsianov (1779–1847), who spent most of his life painting scenes from peasant life. Yet, as Alexander Benois pointed out, Venetsianov's works, though realistic in style, are essentially pictorial, no trace of narrative appearing in them. Venetsianov was a true, if artistically somewhat limited artist. He was the first to try to capture the poetry of the immense fields of Russia, with the peasants busily engaged on their seasonal tasks (*Ill. 213*); he depicted them with a tenderness and impressive simplicity which find their parallels in Pushkin's evocations of country life. Venetsianov had been a pupil of Borovikovski from whom he learnt to delight in simplicity and forthrightness. It was in order to counter the Academy's stultifying influence that he founded a school designed to encourage freedom of expression—a cry which was to be sounded again and again in the latter half of the nineteenth century. Unfortunately, the world-wide success scored by Brüllov's picture of *The Last Day of Pompeii* induced many of Venetsianov's pupils to desert him. Count Tolstoy, a kinsman of the famous writer (1783–1873), was one of the few who remained faithful to Venetsianov and the latter's ideals. Tolstoy was primarily a sculptor and medallist, but he combined something of Alexander Ivanov's interest in character with Venetsianov's concern for actuality; as a result he succeeded in producing some of the best Russian pictures of interiors—a type of

213 *Peasant children in a Field*, by Venetsianov, 1820. Venetsianov devoted himself to painting peasant life, achieving the peaceful atmosphere which distinguishes genre painting from narrative or purpose art

painting which was very popular in Russia towards the end of the Romantic period. His paintings are well composed, they are fresh and vivid, and they abound in contemporary details.

By the middle of the nineteenth century it had, however, become difficult for thinking people to disregard the social evils of the day.

214 *A Poor Aristocrat's Breakfast*, by Fedotov. Fedotov was a child of his age, sharing the satirical spirit of Gogol whilst expressing himself somewhat in the manner of Hogarth. Here the poor aristocrat lives in squalor whilst an advertisement for oysters lies on the chair placed to the left of the picture

The Pugachev Rising of 1773–75 and the French Revolution had already stirred the conscience of a large section of society; the heroic conduct of the Russian troops during the Napoleonic Wars had led Russian officers to appreciate the peasant's many qualities and to realize the poverty in which he lived. Pushkin and Lermontov had fanned the sentiments which led to the Decembrist Rising into the critical spirit which made artists and intellectuals acutely conscious of the bitter injustice and social inequalities that existed throughout the country. In the artistic field the growth of a social conscience led people to turn against the mawkish sentimentality and listless moodiness of the Romantics in favour of realism. The first to strike a blow at the Romantics was a disillusioned army officer called P. A. Fedotov (1815–52), who had begun to paint at the age of thirty. Lacking the necessary training, and fully aware of his technical limitations, perhaps to some extent inspired by the bitter satirical paintings of Alexis Orlovski (1777–1832), Fedotov whiled away his last few years in expressing in paint his disenchantment and boredom with life

215 *A Monastic Refectory*, by Perov, 1865–75. Here the satirical spirit is carried to the point of caricature by this 'purpose' artist's determination to draw attention to existing abuses

(*Ill. 214*). His commentaries on its grim and dreary realities, though earlier in date than any of Chekhov's literary works, are pictorial complements to the latter.

In the visual field it was relatively easy for painters such as Fedotov and Orlovski to attract attention, for architecture, which of all the arts lies nearest to the Russian genius, had entered on a period of decline as the first half of the century drew to a close. The turn had come for literature and music to express the national genius. As a result the visual sphere was left empty at the very time when the middle classes had begun to take an interest in painting, and art was on the way to becoming fashionable. Young men of birth, such as Count Tolstoy, were beginning to turn to painting as a profession; and the Academy was opening its portals to the would-be professional

216 Portrait of a Miller, by Kramskoi. This sincere, competent yet somewhat pedestrian painting is characteristic of the work produced by foremost artists belonging to the Society of Wandering Exhibitions

and the amateur alike. This step was not considered ill advised, for it is only in our own day, as Chesterton remarked, that 'the word (amateur) has come by a thousand oddities of language to convey an idea of tepidity; whereas the word itself has the meaning of passion. . . .' Yet many thinking people felt with Pisarev, who, writing as far back as 1807, affirmed that 'the purpose of art consists in preaching morality so as to raise the spirit of the people'. Vasili Perov (1833–82) was one of those who was influenced both by Fedotov's realistic and Pisarev's moral views, as well as by the growing agitation in favour of the liberation of the serfs. Deserting portraiture for genre he turned his attention to the life of the peasantry, producing realistic, often somewhat satirical though unimaginative, paintings which, as much on account of their content as their aesthetic approach, attracted considerable attention (*Ill. 215*).

It was as a result of the Academy's decision in 1863 to set the theme of Odin in Valhalla as the subject for the annual gold medal award that purpose painting supplanted realistic painting. Thirteen students were so profoundly angered by the Academy's choice of a theme entirely divorced from actuality that they resigned from the Academy and formed themselves into an independent group. In 1870, with I. Kramskoi (1837–87) as their leader, they founded a society, which they called the Society of Wandering Exhibitions, because they intended showing pictures painted in a realistic style with the purpose of advocating social reforms to the country at large by means of travelling exhibitions. Kramskoi was the most mature, as well as the most talented and vigorous of the Wanderers, as the society's members came to be called; indeed, he was soon as well known for his passionate articles as for his precise, carefully observed paintings. His portraits are very competent works (*Ill. 216*), but many of his subject pictures lack atmosphere; not so the one entitled *Inspecting the old house*. With its desolate, nostalgic air, its furniture swathed in dust-sheets, its chandelier hidden in wrappings, the hesitant visitors standing hushed, listening to the crumbling past—it is as if, outside, the cherry orchard was being felled.

The Crimean War and the diplomatic developments resulting from it had had the effect of dividing Russian intellectuals into two groups: those who considered it advisable for Russia to develop along West European lines were known as Westerners, whilst those who believed that it would be better for the country to draw her strength and inspiration from native sources were known as Slavophiles. The origins of the Slavophile movement may well have been laid as far back as the year 1775, when the text of the greatest of all Russian medieval epics, the twelfth-century *Lay of Igor's Men*, was discovered. It encouraged followers of the great writer and thinker M. Lomonosov (1711–65) to take steps to promote higher education throughout the country, an aim in which they were warmly seconded by the poet B. Zhukovski (1783–1852), the tutor of the future Alexander II (1855–81), and the man who implanted in the young Prince the humanitarian views which resulted in 1861 in the emancipation of the serfs. It was largely due to efforts of progressive people such as these that a number of provincial universities came into being and that new interests led to the creation in 1842 of an archaeological society in the capital, and in 1864 of a similar society in Moscow. Others followed in the more important provincial towns, in their turn resulting in the founding of museums, such as the Historical Museum in Moscow (1834–83) or the Archaeological at Kerch. These developments aroused considerable interest, and private individuals began to study the country's antiquities and ancient monuments. Amongst the first to do so was Count Anatoli Demidov, who set out in 1839, accompanied by an artist, to record the architectural monuments of Western Russia. By the 1850s and 1860s scholars had begun to do likewise. The publication by A. Martinov and I. Snegirev of their findings in volumes illustrated with colour plates won such warm commendations that the Academy of Sciences decided to sponsor the publication of V. V Suslov's works on ancient Russian architecture and painting. The undertaking took from 1895 to 1912 to complete, but the books still rank as indispensable standard works. D. Rovinski (1824–95) was, however, the first scholar to devote himself to the study of Russian icons; his findings electrified the Russian art world and were doubtless at any rate in part responsible for the decision of such eminent scholars of the future as N. Kondakov (1844–1925) and N. Likhachev (1862–1935) to concentrate on the same field of study. Their work in its turn helped to mould the taste of such discerning arts lovers as I. Ostroukhov and P. Riabushinski, leading them to form the truly remarkable collections of Russian icons which are now preserved in Russia's leading museums.

Logic as well as sentiment forced the purpose artists and many realists to join the Slavophiles. Some of them developed into narrow-minded nationalists, others remained painstakingly factual, but N. Gey (1831–94), a disciple of Kramskoi, was the antithesis of his leader for, unlike most of the Wanderers, he devoted himself to painting religious pictures. Yet, notwithstanding his profound sincerity, he soon began overloading them with a somewhat mawkish sentimentality, and this gradual dulling of his critical faculties came to be reflected in his growing preference for dim, muted colours. Today, as in the case of Kramskoi, it is his portraits which seem to constitute the more valuable side of his work. Surikov, who was a keen supporter of the Wanderers, or I. Repin (1844–1930) who, though never an active member, was nevertheless deeply influenced

217 *Leo Tolstoy at work,* a portrait in water-colour by Repin. Though academic in style this is a profound, admirably executed work

by Kramskoi and his followers, never confined their pictorial renderings within the bounds of a narrative interpretation; nor were all the Slavophiles uncompromising antiquarians. The munificent Muscovite art patron P. M. Tretyakov (1832–98), whose collection forms the nucleus of Moscow's magnificent museum of Russian art, was a great admirer of living artists, and he not only purchased many of their works, but even subsidized Kramskoi so as to enable him to maintain and expand the activities of the Wanderers.

By and large, in contrast to Moscow, the aristocratic and intellectual circles of St Petersburg tended to favour the Westerners rather than the Slavophiles. Under the impact of these divergent policies and of the ever-growing interest in cultural matters, artistic life in the capital acquired great complexity and vitality, though

235

218 *They did not expect him*, an oil-painting by Repin, 1884. In this work and several others of a similar character Repin produced pictures of aesthetic quality which were also an indictment of existing abuses. This one illustrates the unexpected return from Siberia of a political exile

artists who were primarily concerned with their painting stood somewhat aloof from the turmoil. This was especially true of Repin, whose overriding interest in people led him to devote most of his time to painting his contemporaries (*Ill. 217*). Practically everybody of importance sat for Repin, who recorded their appearance in restrained and severe colours, which are, however, as expressive as are those of Whistler and as such differ completely in character from the sombre and uninteresting colours used by many of the Wanderers. In Repin the colours are a reflection of his mood, for, like so many of his contemporaries, he too was often grieved by the darkening outlook. He expressed his dislike of oppression in some

219 *Girls*, detail from an oil-painting by Malyavin. Painted in deep yet vivid reds and blues this picture, like all Malyavin's works, succeeds in vividly evoking village life in the opening decades of the present century

subject paintings. The finest of these is a picture he painted in 1884, entitled *They did not expect him* (*Ill. 218*); it illustrates the return of a political exile from Siberia. It is a poignant, profound, and extremely convincing psychological study, as well as a painting of real aesthetic merit. The no less sincere and aesthetically equally important painting which is generally known by the name of *The Volga Boatmen* is likewise concerned in drawing attention to a social evil. It is the tragedy of both Surikov and Repin, who were artists of quite unusual ability, that their outlook and styles were formed at a time when it was considered more important for artists to point a moral than to give form to a vision.

Surikov, like Repin or the pacifist Vereshchagin, held aloof from active politics, though he often expressed his political opinions and sympathies in his choice of subject. An important artist to remain unaffected by political issues was P. Malyavin (1869–1939). Of peasant stock, at the age of fourteen Malyavin persuaded his parents to allow him to become a lay brother at the Russian Monastery on Mount Athos. He was discovered there six years later by a visiting academician, who sent the youth back to St Petersburg to study at the Academy. Malyavin (*Ill. 219*) became an elegant draughtsman and an able portrait painter, but there was something primeval about his character, and he sought release for his earthier and more exuberant impressions in a series of pictures of Russian peasant women aswirl in red fustian. Painted with nervous brush-strokes not unlike those used by followers of Theophanes the Greek, his famous picture of a peasant woman entitled *The Red Laugh* may indeed have been to some degree prophetic.

Under Alexander II and Alexander III, P. P. Chistyakov (1832–1919), a teacher at the Academy and a painter in his own right, was the great formative influence. He was not a revolutionary, but he passionately believed in the importance of individualism controlled by severe self-criticism. Most of the leading painters of the day passed through his hands in their youth, and he was thus able to exert his influence over artists of the calibre of Surikov, Repin, Vrubel, Serov, Polenov and Vasnetsov. Mikhail Vrubel (1856–1910) in fact became Russia's first individualist, as well as one of her foremost

220 *The Bogatyr*, a decorative panel by Vrubel, 1898. The *bogatyr*—the heroic knight of folk-lore, more than life-size in his person, superhuman in his achievements—epitomized for the Russians their ability to withstand alike the human enemy and the malevolent spirits

221 *Girl with Peaches*, by Serov, 1887. Painted during what the artist termed the happiest year of his life, immediately upon his return to Abramtzevo from Italy, this portrait of Vera Savishna Mamontova is bathed in sunshine and serenity

artists (*Ill. 220*). A tragic and profoundly sincere genius, Vrubel was always haunted by strange visions which eventually led him to end his days in a lunatic asylum. These visions were often tinged with a touch of Blake's mysticism and of Poe's horror. Because they fail to reflect the influence of the French Impressionists, outside Russia they tend today to rank with nineteenth-century academic paintings, yet they contain an imaginative intensity, and a sense of form and colour which unbiased critics cannot fail to recognize as truly

222 Portrait of Nicholas II, by Serov, 1900. It is seldom that a portrait of a sovereign is also a character study. In his *Catherine the Great walking her dog* Borovikovski produced an unusually intimate picture, but psychologically it falls far short of this

inspired. In Russia Vrubel's works were the first to point to a new goal—that of art for art's sake rather than of art as a means to freedom of expression. Of all the painters working in the last decades of the nineteenth century it was perhaps V. Serov (1865–1911) who, whilst continuing to paint in a conventional style, was the first to realize this.

Serov was primarily a portraitist, and even though he was fond of painting landscapes, he will in time come to be recognized as an outstanding portrait painter. Surikov had shown him the value of fine colours, a lesson which the revived interest in icons had helped to stress. It was from these ancient panels that Serov also became aware of the significance of the essential in a composition and the unimportance of the unnecessary, but it was undoubtedly Vrubel who showed Serov the value of responding to a personal emotional experience. Serov was thus able to make his mark at the age of twenty-two on exhibiting two paintings, *Girl with Peaches* (*Ill. 221*) and *Girl in Sunlight*. At the time of painting them he was unfamiliar with the works of the French Impressionists, yet he came very close to Renoir in these luminous, sunny, splendidly composed portraits (*Ill. 222*). However, Diaghilev's inclusion in his 1905 exhibition of Russian art of a large number of portraits by Levitski made so deep an impression on Serov, who had seen Levitski's paintings only singly, that he forsook his gay colours for the sombre ones which he associated with the older master, and these were attuned to the ever-darkening political situation. It was thus that Serov's earlier works were responsible for heralding the new age which is associated with the World of Art movement, which a younger generation of artists instigated; but the later works lost none of their intrinsic aesthetic value by the change in Serov's style.

Meanwhile, whilst some Russians were turning to antiquarianism, and whilst Vrubel and Serov were leading the next generation of artists towards a new goal, businessmen of a new type were endeavouring to transform Russia into a modern industrial State. The decorative arts had been steadily losing ground since the country's westernization, and folk art had tended to mark time at the precise moment when a section of the community had come to realize its worth. Quick to appreciate industry's threat to craftsmanship, this group set out to encourage cottage industries by appointing the sensitive artist Marya Yakunchikova organizer of the craft centres which they were anxious to establish in the towns and the workshops they wanted to set up in the rural areas. Wealthier patrons came forward to provide wider facilities by founding workshops on their estates in which the craftsmen could benefit from the advice of leading artists. Among the more important of these foundations

223 Abramtzevo, Savva Mamontov's country house near Moscow, was the place where far-reaching steps were taken by the owner both to encourage artists to express themselves and to ensure the survival of rural craftsmanship

were the workshops which Princess Tenisheva established in the 1890s on her estate at Talashkino, near Smolensk, where tuition in choral singing was available to craftsmen engaged on producing pottery, embroidery, and textiles; the Cholokhov carpet factory also offered vocational training to its workers and the Stroganovs went to the length of founding a technical institute. But perhaps even more far reaching in their results were the experiments carried out at Abramtzevo (*Ill. 223*), a country house near Moscow in which Aksakov and Gogol had lived; it was purchased in the 1870s by the Muscovite merchant-prince Savva Mamontov. Mamontov was an astonishingly munificent and imaginative patron of the arts. On acquiring Abramtzevo he came under the joint influence of William Morris's teaching and of *avant-garde* circles in Munich with the result that he persuaded his guests at Abramtzevo, who invariably included a number of distinguished artists, to help in building, decorating, and adorning a new village church. Among the guests were the Slavophile artists Victor Vasnetsov (1848–1926) (*Ill. 224*) and Vasili Polenov (1844–1927), as well as the latter's sister, Vera, and her friend Marya Yakunchikova. Their corporate efforts were brought

224 *A Warrior at the Crossroads*, by V. Vasnetsov, 1882. In response to Slavophile influence Vasnetsov turned largely to folk-lore for the subjects of his pictures; like Vrubel he found fruitful inspiration in the epics telling of the deeds of valour performed by warriors of long ago

to a successful close in 1882, but the experience had proved so rewarding that Mamontov decided to establish at Abramtzevo workshops in which pottery, much of it reflecting the influence of Art Nouveau, and various forms of applied art were taught and practised under the supervision of Marya Yakunchikova. Many leading artists of the day, including Vrubel, furnished these workshops with designs, and as a result the objects produced in them were so distinctive that they left their mark on the decorative arts of pre-Revolutionary Russia. Indeed, the alliance of craftsmanship and art may well have had more far-reaching effects than is realized, contributing perhaps to the birth of Constructivist art in the second decade of the present century.

Mamontov's activities were not confined to the workshops at Abramtzevo. His interest in the theatre made him turn to some of the leading artists of the day for the scenery for the operas he produced in his private theatre. His Slavophile sympathies led him to ask V. Vasnetsov in 1882 to design the scenery of *Little Snow-*

225 A sketch-book illustration by Stelletski. Stelletski and his fellow-artist Bilibin were both regarded as leading experts on Russian folk-lore, ethnography, and archaeology. They are seen at their best in graphic art

White, and in 1886 for that of the *Snow Queen*. As in so many of his pictures, the artist gave both a Russian fairy-tale setting which greatly influenced the style of such realist painters as V. E. Makovski (1841–1920) and of younger men such as I. Bilibin (1876–1928) and D. Stelletski (1875–1947) (*Ill. 225*), both of whom spent the rest of their lives working in the style of the late medieval book illuminators. Vasnetsov also affected the young N. Goncharova (1881–1962) and a host of others, perhaps to some extent even the far younger Favorski (*Ill. 226*). More important still was Mamontov's decision to commission scenery from two young Muscovites, K. Korovin (1861–1939) and A. Golovin (1863–1930). Korovin was perhaps the

226 (*above*) *October 1917*, an engraving by Favorski. Favorski is an engraver whose works will always hold an important place in the history of Russian art. Some of his best work has been produced in the USSR since the outbreak of the October Revolution, the subject of which forms the theme of this illustration

227 (*left*) Sketch for a costume for the opera *The tale of the invisible town of Kitezh and the Maiden Fevrosina* by Korovin, 1908. The opera, the music of which was by Rimsky-Korsakov, tells of Russia's fight against the Mongol Khan Batu. The work was first produced in 1907 with settings by A. Vasnetsov, but Korovin was responsible for those for the 1908 revival

more gifted of the two, but Golovin was to prove the greater theatrical artist, for he was the first to realize the importance of making scenery accord with a play's plot, period, and music (*Ill. 228*). Both artists used exciting colours, and because of this they are often described as Impressionists, yet neither was at all interested in the theories of the French painters; in fact, it was precisely because they and their contemporaries remained unaffected by the French Impressionists that the Diaghilev Ballets made so profound an impact on Western Europe, for the Russians were able to suggest new developments which represented a break as well as an advance from Impressionism (*Ill. 227*).

228 Backcloth for the opera *The Nightingale*, by Golovin. Golovin more than anyone else was responsible for transforming stage settings for he was the first to use enchantingly vivid colours in the theatre

229 (*left*) Design for Aurora's wedding-dress in *The Sleeping Princess* by Léon Bakst

230 (*right*) Curtain for Rimsky-Korsakov's *Coq d'Or* by Alexander Benois. Though the idea for Diaghilev's first production of *Coq d'Or* in 1914 came from Benois, the artist was so busy in arranging for the work to be produced in the form of an operatic ballet that he commissioned the scenery from Goncharova. With the years he came to feel that her colourful setting savoured too much of the fairy-tale, and for the 1927 revival at the Paris Opéra he produced this setting of a more archaeological character

In 1898 Mamontov brought his company to St Petersburg. On seeing them Telyakovski was quick to realize that Mamontov had transformed the role of the stage, and one of his first steps on being appointed Director of the Board of the Imperial Theatres was to persuade Korovin and Golovin to establish themselves in the capital in order to work for the Imperial Theatres. In the political ferment created by the Revolution of 1905, first the stage then art exhibitions became as important an outlet for the less belligerent innovators in the artistic field as the writing of manifestoes did for the more active, such as Larionov. A. Benois (1870–1961) and his friends—and these numbered Serge Diaghilev—were devoted to the theatre (*Ill. 230*), but they had wider ambitions and interests. 'Art for Art's sake' was their slogan, and with this aim in view they formed themselves into a society which they called the World of Art. In 1904 Diaghilev

founded the magazine of the same name, the better to express their
opinions. Their importance, both in the cultural and the artistic field,
cannot be overestimated. In addition to its founders, the society soon
numbered among its numerous members such significant painters as
Golovin, Korovin, Bakst (*Ill. 229*), Benois's nephew Lanceré,
Dobuzhinski (*Ill. 232*), whose pupils included Marc Chagall, Yuon
(born 1875) (*Ill. 231*), and many more of those who were to make
their mark in Russia and to take Europe by storm when the Russian
Ballet came to the West in 1909. The society's exhibitions took place
annually from 1899 to 1922, and much that was best in the art of the
period was included in them, but equally important were the great
exhibitions which Diaghilev organized in the capital, starting in 1897
with an exhibition of British water-colours. A year later he followed
it up with one devoted to Scandinavian art, and, after a break of seven

231 *A Sunny Spring Day*, by Yuon, 1904. It is painted in the Neo-classical manner favoured by artists belonging to the World of Art Society. The treatment is to some extent reminiscent of Lowry

years, he arranged one of historic Russian portraits in the splendid setting provided by the Tauride Palace. In 1905 the retrospective exhibition of Russian art, with the assembled works of Levitski as its main feature, created a deep impression not only on Serov, but on the World of Art group as a whole. The publication of illustrated monthlies such as Diaghilev's *World of Art*, *Apollo*, *The Golden Fleece*, and several other magazines of the same calibre served not only to counteract the Art Nouveau influences stemming from the Abramtzevo workshops, but also kept readers informed about developments in the West, devoting particular attention to such innovations as the work of Charles Rennie Mackintosh. In Moscow, however, interest centred on Germany rather than on France and Britain, the influence of the Symbolists in Munich making itself strongly felt from about

232 *Interior*, by M. Dobuzhinski, *c.* 1927. Dobuzhinski was a member of the World of Art Society; his gifts as a colourist and decorator were greatly admired, and although he worked in the Neo-classical style his pictures remain important

1892 onwards. Symbolism finds much of its inspiration in sadness and despondency—it is in fact a form of intellectual romanticism. In Russia it appealed first to Petrov-Vodkin (1878–1939) (*Ill. 233*), but it was Mikhail Larionov (born 1881), warmly seconded by his lifelong companion Natalia Goncharova, as well as by Borissov-Mussatov (1870–1905), who became the most active supporters of a movement which was for a time to include among its exponents the young Chagall. Borissov-Mussatov, an unhappy, lonely person, was the one who most ardently sought escape from life in art, striving, at any rate in his earlier works, to depict nature's life-giving properties rather than its outward forms (*Ill. 234*). Chagall was the most emotional of the group (*Ill. 235*), Larionov the most intellectual, and it was he who probed most passionately into Symbolism,

233 *1918 in Petrograd*, by Petrov-Vodkin, 1920. The artist was fascinated by curves, depending on them to create a sense of space and balance

234 *The Reservoir*, by Borissov-Mussatov, 1902. Under the influence of Puvis de Chavannes the artist expressed both the melancholy which possessed him and his striving towards Symbolism by using deep, sustained colours ranging from blues to soft greys and greens, whilst continuing to paint in a naturalistic manner

expressing himself in a series of brilliantly coloured works which led Diaghilev to invite him to take part in the exhibition of Russian art to be held in Paris in 1906. Diaghilev also included works by other leading Symbolists. Goncharova was among them, having reached this point in her development by way of Vrubel, Vasnetsov, medieval icons, and the peasant *lubok*. As a descendant of Pushkin's she was especially keenly attuned to the sadder aspects of the Russian landscape and the native elements in her country's art; she therefore

235 *Russian Soldiers*, by Chagall, 1917. This splendid early work of the master shows how close the links were which bound him at that time to the group of experimental artists centring round Larionov and Goncharova

236 *Monk with Cat*, by Goncharova, 1910. The symbolic approach is stressed by the use of curved lines derived from medieval icon painting to produce an atmosphere which recalls that of many an early work by Chagall

unconsciously produced flat, silhouette-like figures whose outlines resembled those Rublev had evolved for his mystical interpretations of the Scriptures (*Ill. 240, 241*), outlines which were equally well suited to the mystical outlook of the Symbolists (*Ill. 236*).

Larionov spent from 1906 to 1907 in Paris; he thus missed the important retrospective exhibition of Borissov-Mussatov's work

237 *Soldier in a Wood*, by Larionov, 1908–09. The influence of peasant toys, whether made in wood or in pottery, is to be seen in the figures of the man and his donkey

which Diaghilev, with his innate ability to recognize the significant in art, organized in St Petersburg in 1906. The work of the dead artist helped, however, to focus attention on the paintings and opinions which the living Larionov was expressing in printed manifestoes. On his return to Russia from Paris in 1907 Larionov held his own Symbolist 'Blue Rose' exhibition (*Ill. 237*). In 1909, he was

238 *Man in a Cellar*, by Grigoriev. Grigoriev abandoned the neo-academic style of the World of Art Society to experiment in Cubo-Futurism. His cycle of portraits entitled 'The face of Russia', painted in the same style and at much the same time as *Man in a Cellar*, is of enduring value

conscripted for military duties and it looked as though there would of necessity be a break in his output, yet he contrived whilst in the army to continue his search for a new pictorial idiom. The tubular, angular figures of soldiers at work and at rest in a nebulous, primitivist world date from this period; they foreshadow the rather later works which William Roberts was to produce in England. Already in 1908, assisted by Nikolai Riabushinski, Larionov had been responsible for the first 'Golden Fleece' exhibition, in which the works of French Impressionists and *avant-garde* Russians were hung side by side. A second was held in the following year. Petrov-Vodkin figured in both as a leading Symbolist, and it is profoundly tragic

239 *Cityscape*, by A. Exter, *c.* 1916. From the start of her career in about 1916 the artist was closely associated with Tairov, the Director of the 'Emancipated' theatre performing at Moscow's famous Kamerny Theatre. It was whilst working for him that Exter started feeling her way by means of Cubism towards Abstraction

that, towards the end of his life, this gifted artist was obliged to revert to the stultifying canons of realist art. Meanwhile Larionov and Goncharova had begun to feel their way towards Cubo-Futurism, hoping by its means to convey a feeling of movement in painting. However, their Futurism assumed an essentially Russian form, for they used the medium realistically, turning to geometry in order to attain to the essence of an object rather than so as to endow it, as Western artists tried to do, with a three-dimensional quality. Grigoriev also experimented in this vein, using Cubism Impressionistically (*Ill. 238*), excluding, as in icons, shadows and highlights.

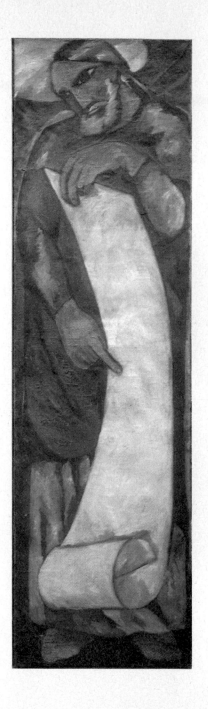

240 (*left*) Icon of the Archangel
Michael; Novgorodian school; sixteenth century. The panel comes from
the Deesis tier of an iconostasis and is
painted in the Rublev tradition. The
Archangel's inclined head and rounded
shoulders, so typical of the Rublev
school, also greatly influenced Goncharova. The extent to which it did so
is to be seen in many of her works, but
is especially obvious in her religious
paintings. The resemblance is very
evident in *Ill. 241* (*right*). This painting
of an Evangelist, was produced by Goncharova in 1910. It is so deeply imbued
with religious feeling that in 1920, when
Goncharova included it in Larionov's
avant-garde 'Donkey's Tail' exhibition,
the authorities objected and obliged her
to withdraw it

242 *Composition from a Nude*, by Tatlin, 1913. Tatlin was the founder of Constructivism. Though he later introduced real materials into his works to create effects of real space, in his earlier works he was much influenced by the curved lines of medieval icon painting as well as by the flat surfaces

Larionov's determination to find a new form of painting underlay the 'Knave of Diamonds' exhibition which he organized in 1910. His striving for a new idiom won him the support of Borissov-Mussatov's pupil Kusnetsov, of Lissitski, and of Yakulov, who was in 1927 to produce the Constructivist settings for Diaghilev's ballet *Le Pas*

243 Portrait of the artist Vladimir Tatlin, by Larionov, 1913–14. Painted in the artist's Cubo-Rayonnist manner, the interplay of the rays, reinforced as they are by the shadow thrown by the figure's body, help to give substance to the portrait whilst creating a sense of space

d'Acier. Martinos, Saroyan, Utkin, the Futurist painter Exter (*Ill. 239*), and David Burlyuk (born 1882) also took part in the exhibition. More important still was the gradual enticement of Kandinski from the neo-academic World of Art group, and the participation of Jawlensky, Tatlin (*Ill. 242*), and Malevich in the 'Donkey's Tail' exhibition which Larionov organized in Moscow to mark the group's break with the French school of painting and its determination to evolve a national style based on native sources.

With Kandinski (*Ill. 245*), Larionov attached immense importance to the precise moment of inspiration; this view led him to form the new conception of painting which he defined as Rayonnism (*Ill. 243*). It expressed Larionov's efforts to penetrate to the essence of an object, for in his search for this essence he came to perceive rays emanating from objects. He traced these rays till they encountered those produced by another object, marking their meeting-point by a haze of colour which came to form the main subject of his paintings. Larionov's earliest experiment in this vein dates from 1911 when he set out to trace the rays linking a mackerel to a sausage. Later he

244 *Yellow Quadrilateral on White*, by Malevich, 1916–17. Larionov's Rayonnist theories helped Malevich to evolve the Suprematist conceptions which he expressed in linear or abstract compositions, leading him to feel that basic form alone was truly significant

245 *Composition No. 2*, by Kandinski, 1910. By using spots of colour and linear outlines Kandinski has produced a series of rhythmical, balanced forms of a semi-abstract character which successfully expresses an entirely personal vision

followed the rays associating groups of objects and the colours which they formed at their points of contact inspired his pure as distinct from abstract pictures, for abstract painting is an attempt by the artist to represent his ideas and reactions to a given subject, not, as in Rayonnism, to convey an impression of the colour images evoked by a given subject. This line of thought was surely not disregarded by Nicholas de Staël when, several decades later, he grappled with the problems of images and self-expression.

Whilst Larionov was experimenting with Rayonnism other artists, notably the Pevsner brothers, who are better known today respectively as Antoine Pevsner and Naum Gabo, using French Cubism as

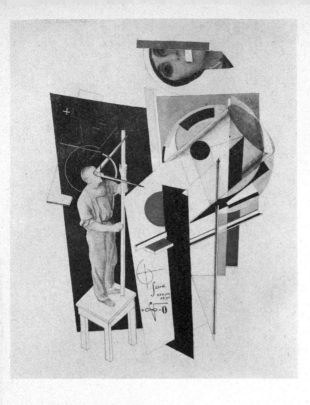

246 (*left*) Tatlin working on the Monument of the Third International, by El Lissitski who believed in the artist's right to use mechanical devices or photography to create works of art which, though not reproduceable by machinery, would have meaning for people living in a machine age distinguished by standardization in all objects other than works of art

247 (*below*) Setting for Diaghilev's ballet *La Chatte*, by Pevsner and Naum Gabo. In the years following the outbreak of the Revolution Tairov launched Constructivism on the stage of the Kamerny Theatre; the style was taken over by Germany and in 1927 Diaghilev produced ballets with Constructivist settings

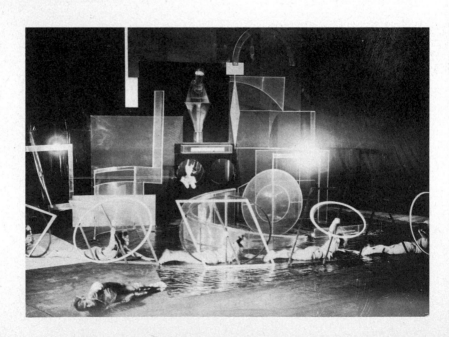

248 (*above*) *Skulpturmalerei*, by Archipenko, 1915. Michael Ayrton has explained how at times a sculptor feels obliged to express an idea in paint and a painter in sculpture. Here the sculptor has invested three-dimensional forms with the plastic characteristics which could only be expressed in paint

249 (*right*) *Construction 1922*, by Naum Gabo. Gabo reached Constructivism through geometric forms which he first applied to representations of the human figure. These failed to satisfy his preoccupation with move-ment—admirably mastered in this study of forms

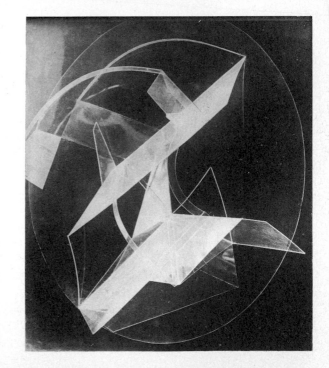

their starting-point, possibly working too with the feeling for crafts-manship encouraged at Abramtzevo, evolved in conjunction with Malevich the Constructivist theories (*Ill. 247*) which attracted more attention in Paris than did Larionov's Rayonnism. Naum Gabo's three-dimensional constructions in wire and other materials, with their blend of architectural and plastic forms interpreted in a graphic manner were designed to express a 'synthesis of the plastic arts' (*Ill. 249*). El Lissitski (1890–1941) became a great exponent of this type of work. Its effect on the Russian stage was very considerable, some of the more interesting plays of the opening years of the Revolution being produced in Constructivist settings. The finest works were created by Malevich (*Ill. 244*) and Lissitski (*Ill. 246*), both of whom were able to participate in the Russian exhibition organized in Berlin in 1922, when they established warm contacts with the Bauhaus group. Under their influence the revived interest in sculp-ture, first fostered by Vrubel, who was also a distinguished sculptor, and by the World of Art group of artists, led to experiments in self-expression which enabled sculptors such as Archipenko (*Ill. 248*) and Lipchitz to bring this form of art to a high level, and to create works the influence of which still continues to make itself felt in Western Europe.

Larionov and Goncharova left Russia in 1915 to join Diaghilev in Paris; they never returned to their native land. Many of the World of Art artists also forsook their homeland in the 1920s. Men like Benois, Dobuzhinski, Sorin, Shukhaev (*Ill. 250*), Sudeikin (*Ill. 251*), and Yakovlev were among many others whose works were so greatly admired in the countries in which they made their homes that many were bought for Europe's foremost museums, yet—by and large—divorced from their homeland, the momentum of these artists slackened. Nor did those who, like Yuon, Igor Grabar, Petrov-Vodkin, or Golovin, to name but a few, stayed in Russia, fare much better, for although they too continued to be appreciated, they eventually came to conform with the new ideology's demand for essentially realistic records of life instead of interpretations of visual and emotional experiences. Because this represents a negation of art the advance which their generation had done so much to foster

250 (*right*) *Women Bathing*, by Shukhaev. On emigrating from Russia as a result of the Revolution, Shukhaev was for a time profoundly influenced both by Gauguin and by Negro art, but the interest which many of his friends took in curved lines continued to pervade his works

251 (*below*) *Russian Toys*, by Sudeikin. Sudeikin produced this charming oil-painting in a moment of homesickness soon after emigrating from Russia as a result of the Revolution. It is an evocative synthesis of all that was gay and charming in peasant life, and that had disappeared for ever before pleasures of a new sort

petered out, and their later output, for all its technical accomplishment, proved sterile, and failed to help young artists to find fresh images to suit a new age. Only when the canvases of the artists who were working during the first decades of the twentieth century are assembled in their rightful places on the walls of Russia's museums will the importance of the World of Art painters, and foremost among them of Benois, Bakst, and Dobuzhinski be generally realized. It was they and their followers who covered the last lap of an immensely long journey, and with but few exceptions it was they and their friends who produced paintings which can hold their own beside the medieval masterpieces, and which at the same time disclose new vistas to the rising generation of Russian artists.

Some Significant Dates

860	First Slav attack launched against Constantinople
862	Varangian princes invited to rule over the Slavs
862–79	Reign of Prince Rurik in Novgorod
907	Oleg's campaign against Byzantium
957	Olga visits Constantinople
988–89	Vladimir adopts Christianity as the official religion
1015	Death of the Grand Duke Vladimir
1019–54	Reign of the Grand Duke Yaroslav the Wise
1113–25	Reign of Vladimir Monomachus in Kiev
1147	First reference to Moscow in a chronicle
1157	Death of Yuri Dolgoruki
1174	Death of Andrei Bogolyubski
1212	Death of Grand Duke Vsevolod III of Vladimir-Suzdal
1237–38	The Mongols invade Russia under Batu
1240	Fall of Kiev to the Mongol Tartars Victory of Prince Alexander Nevski over the Swedes
1242	Victory of Prince Alexander Nevski over the Teutonic Order
1263	Death of Prince Alexander Nevski
1325–41	Ivan I Kalita
1328	The Metropolitan moves his see from Vladimir to Moscow
1353–59	Ivan II (of Moscow)
1359–89	Prince Dmitri Donskoi
1380	Defeat of the Mongols on the field of Kulikovo by Dmitri Donskoi
1389–1425	Vasili I
1425–62	Vasili II
1462–1505	Ivan III
1472	Marriage of Ivan III to Sophia Paleologa
1478	Moscow annexes Novgorod
1480	Overthrow of Mongol rule
1485	Moscow annexes Tver (Kalinin)
1510	Moscow annexes Pskov
1514	Moscow annexes Smolensk
1533–84	Reign of Ivan IV, the Terrible
1547	Marriage and coronation of Ivan IV Fire of Moscow
1550–51	Council of the Stoglav (or the Hundred Chapters)
1552	Conquest of Kazan
1556	Conquest of Astrakhan
1582	Conquest of Siberia
1584–98	Tsar Fedor
1589	The Metropolitan is raised to the rank of patriarch
1591	Murder of Prince Dmitri at Uglich
1598	End of the dynasty of Ivan Kalita. Coronation of Boris Godunov
1605	Death of Godunov and beginning of a period of unrest
1613	Mikhail Romanov elected to the throne
1645–76	Tsar Alexis
1652–58	Nikon as patriarch institutes his reforms

1672	Birth of Peter the Great		1730–40	Empress Anna
1676–82	Reign of Feodor, Peter's half-brother		1740–41	Emperor Ivan VI
1682–89	Sophia regent, with Peter first as co-ruler and then as tsar		1741–62	Empress Elizabeth
			1762	Peter III
1697–99	Peter's travels in Western Europe		1762–96	Catherine II, the Great
1700	Abolition of the patriarchate		1796–1801	Paul I
1703	Peter founds St Petersburg		1801–25	Alexander I
1707	St Petersburg succeeds Moscow as capital of Russia		1825–55	Nicholas I
			1855–81	Alexander II
1721	Peter assumes the title of emperor		1861	Emancipation of the serfs
1725	Death of Peter		1881–94	Alexander III
1725–27	Catherine I		1894–1917	Nicholas II
1727–30	Peter II		1917	Outbreak of the Revolution

Selected Bibliography

ALPATOV, M. V. *Altrussische Ikonen Malerei* Dresden, 1938

ALPATOV, M. V. *Universal History of Art* (in Russian) 10 vols, Moscow, 1955

ALPATOV, M. V., ed. *Art Treasures of the Kremlin* (in Russian) Moscow, 1956

ALPATOV, M. V. *Andrei Rublev* (in Russian) Moscow, 1959

AVIROFF, A. *American icons and objects of ecclesiastical and decorative arts from the collection of G. R. Hann* Pittsburg, 1944

BENOIS, A. *The Russian School of Painting* London, 1919

BENOIS, A. *Reminiscences of the Russian Ballet* London, 1941

BERDYAEV, N. A. *The Russian Idea* London, 1947

BRUNOV, N. I. and ALPATOV, M. V. *Geschichte der Altrussischen Kunst* 2 vols, Augsburg, 1932

BUNT, C. G. E. *Russian Art from Scyths to Soviets* London, 1946

BUXTON, D. R. *Russian Mediaeval Architecture* Cambridge, 1934

FARBMAN, M., ed. *Masterpieces of Russian Painting* London, 1930

GRABAR, I., ed. 1st edition, *History of Russian Art* (in Russian), 6 vols, Moscow, 1910–15; 2nd edition, Moscow, 1940

GRAY, C. *The Great Experiment: Russian Art, 1863–1922* London, 1962

GREKOV, B. D. and ARTAMONOV, M. I., ed. *A History of the Culture of Ancient Russia* (in Russian) 1958; rev. ed., 1951

HAMILTON, G. H. *The Art and Architecture of Russia* Harmondsworth, 1954

HASKELL, A. *Diaghileff, his Artistic and Private Life* London, 1935

HURLIMANN, M. *Moscow and Leningrad* London, 1959

KARGER, M. K., ed. *Ancient Kiev* (in Russian) 1951

KONDAKOV, N. P. *Die russische Ikone* (in Russian) Prague, 1928–33; trans. Minns, E. H. *The Russian Icon* (abridged text) Oxford, 1927

LAZAREV, V. *The Art of Novgorod* (in Russian), 2 vols, Moscow, 1947

LAZAREV, V. *Andrei Rublev* (in Russian) Moscow, 1960; (Summary and captions also in Eng., Fr., and Ger.)

LAZAREV, V. *The Mosaics of the Cathedral of St Sophia, Kiev* (in Russian) Moscow, 1960

LAZAREV, V. *Theophanes the Greek* (in Russian) Moscow, 1962

LIKHACHEV, D. S. *The Individual in the Literature of Ancient Russia* (in Russian) 1958

LIKHACHEV, N. P. *Matériaux pour l'histoire de l'ikonographie russe* (Material for the History of Russian Icon Painting), plates only; vol. I, Plates I–CCX, St Petersburg, 1906; vol. II, Plates CCXI–CCCCXIX, Paris–St Petersburg, 1906–08

LO GATTO, E. *Gli Artisti italiani in Russia*, 3 vols, Rome, 1934

LUKOMSKI, G. K. *Alt-Russland. Architektur und Kunstgewerbe* Munich, 1923

LUKOMSKI, G. K. *L'art décoratif russe* Paris, 1928

LUKOMSKI, G. K. *La Vie et les mœurs en Russie. De Pierre le Grand à Lénine* Paris, 1928

LUKOMSKI, G. K. *Mobilier et décoration des anciens palais impériaux russes* Paris, 1928

LUKOMSKI, G. K. *L'architecture religieuse russe du XIe au XVIIe siècle* Paris, 1929

LUKOMSKI, G. K. *Le Kremlin de Moscou* Paris, 1940

LUKOMSKI, G. K. *Charles Cameron, 1740–1812* London, 1943

MARSDEN, C. *Palmyra of the North. The First Days of St Petersburg* London, 1942

MONGAIT, A. L. *Archaeology in the USSR* Harmondsworth, 1951

MURATOV, P. *Les icones russes* Paris, 1927

MURATOV, P. *Trente-cinq primitifs russes* Paris, 1931

REAU, L. *L'art russe des origines à Pierre le Grand* Paris, 1921

REAU, L. *L'art russe de Pierre le Grand à nos jours* Paris, 1922

Recklinghausen Publications on icons:
BIEDERMANN, H. M. *Die Passion* 1958
FABRICIUS, U. *Jesus Christ* 1957
GERHARD, H. P. *Muttergottes* 1956
LOESCHCKE, W. *Apostel und Evangelisten* 1958

RICE, D. TALBOT *Russian Icons* Harmondsworth, 1947

RICE, T. TALBOT *Russian Art* Harmondsworth, 1949

RICE, T. TALBOT *The Scythians* London, 1957

RICE, T. TALBOT *Icons* London, 1958

SITWELL, S. *Valse de fleurs* London, 1941

Studio Publication *Peasant Art* London, 1912

SUSLOV, V. V. *Monuments de l'art ancien russe* (in Russian) St Petersburg, 1908–12

SUSLOV, V. V. *Monuments de l'ancienne architecture russe* (in Russian) St Petersburg, 1895–1901

TOLSTOY, I. I. and KONDAKOV, N. P. *Russian antiquities and monuments of art* (in Russian), 6 vols, St Petersburg, 1889–99

TSCHIGEWSKIJ, D. *Das heilige Russland*, vol. I, Hamburg, 1959

TSCHIGEWSKIJ, D. *Zwischen Ost und West*, vol. II, Hamburg, 1961

VOYCE, A. *The Moscow Kremlin* London, 1955

WULFF, O. and ALPATOV, M. *Denkmäler der Ikonenmalerei* Hellerau, 1925

List of Illustrations

The author and publishers are grateful to the many official bodies, institutions, and individuals mentioned below for their assistance in supplying original illustration material

1 Map of Russia. Drawn by Shalom Shotten

2 Illuminated initial dated to 1346 from a Gospel in the USSR State Public Library. Photo: Gasilov, Leningrad

3 12th-century silver bangle from the Historical Museum, Moscow. After Alpatov

4 7th-century bronze clasp from the Historical Museum, Moscow. After Alpatov

5 6th-century cast silver amulet from the Historical Museum, Kiev

6 Plan of the Cathedral of Hagia Sophia, Kiev, 1036–46. After Alpatov

7 West front of the Cathedral of Hagia Sophia, Kiev, as it appears today. Photo: Courtauld Institute, London

8 Reconstruction of the west front of Hagia Sophia, Kiev, as it appeared in the 11th century. After Alpatov

9 11th-century mosaic of St Basil the Great from the Cathedral of Hagia Sophia, Kiev

10 11th-century mosaic of St Demetrius, from the Mikhailov-Zlatoverkh Monastery, Kiev, now in the Tretyakov Gallery, Moscow. $87\frac{3}{4} \times 52\frac{1}{2}$ (223 × 131). Photo: Gasilov, Leningrad

11 11th-century fresco of the daughters of the Grand Duke Yaroslav in the Cathedral of Hagia Sophia, Kiev

12 11th-century fresco of a secular entertainment from the Cathedral of Hagia Sophia, Kiev

13 11th-century fresco of a musician from the Cathedral of Hagia Sophia, Kiev

14 Icon of the Virgin of Svensk, 13th century, Tretyakov Gallery, Moscow. $26\frac{3}{8} \times 16\frac{1}{2}$ (67 × 42). Photo: Gasilov, Leningrad

15 The Church of the Saviour at Pereyaslavl-Zalessk, 1152. Photo: Gasilov, Leningrad

16 The south front of the Cathedral of St Dmitri, Vladimir, 1194–97. Photo: Sally Crosse

17 Plan of the Cathedral of St George, Yuriev-Polski. After Alpatov

18 The Cathedral of St George, Yuriev-Polski, 1230–34. Photo: Gasilov, Leningrad

19–23 Details of sculptures from the Cathedral of St George, Yuriev-Polski. Photos: Gasilov, Leningrad

24 Drawn thread work from Nizhni-Novgorod (Gorki). Early 19th century

25 Miniature showing a Council of Bishops from the Svyatoslav Codex, 1073. USSR State Public Library. Photo: L'Œil, Paris

26 Byzantine icon of the *Virgin of Vladimir*, 12th century. Tretyakov Gallery, Moscow. $44\frac{1}{2} \times 26\frac{3}{4}$ (113 × 68). Photo: Thames and Hudson archive

27 Icon of the Vernicle, 12th century. Tretyakov Gallery, Moscow. $30 \times 27\frac{3}{4}$ (76·4 × 70·5). Photo: Gasilov, Leningrad

28 Icon of the Adoration of the Cross, 12th century. Tretyakov Gallery, Moscow. Photo: Gasilov, Leningrad

29 Icon of the *Ustyug Annunciation*, 12th century. Tretyakov Gallery, Moscow. $92\frac{1}{2} \times 67\frac{1}{2}$ (235 × 169). After *Peinture de l'Ancienne Russie*

30 Icon of the Archangel Gabriel, 12th century. Russian Museum, Leningrad. $19\frac{1}{4} \times 15\frac{1}{2}$ (49 × 38·7)

31 Icon of the Virgin Orans, 12th–13th century. $76\frac{3}{4} \times 48\frac{3}{8}$ (192×122). Tretyakov Gallery, Moscow

32 Icon of St Demetrius of Salonica, 12th century. $62\frac{1}{2} \times 43\frac{1}{2}$ (156×109). Tretyakov Gallery, Moscow

33 Detail from an icon of the Deesis, 12th century. $31\frac{1}{2} \times 51\frac{1}{2}$ (79×129). Tretyakov Gallery, Moscow. After *Peinture de l'Ancienne Russie*

34 Icon of the Deesis, 13th century. Tretyakov Gallery, Moscow. Photo: Gasilov, Leningrad

35 Detail from a fresco of the Last Judgement, Vladimir, 12th century. Photo: Gasilov, Leningrad

36 Detail from a fresco of the Last Judgement, Vladimir, 1408. Photo: Gasilov, Leningrad

37 Panel from the west door of Suzdal Cathedral, 1222–33. After Alpatov

38 Marginal design from the 16th-century Gospel. Egerton 3. British Museum, London. Photo: Eileen Tweedy

39 East front of the Cathedral of Hagia Sophia, Novgorod, 1045–52. Photo: Gasilov, Leningrad

40 Church of St George in the Yuriev Monastery, Novgorod, 1119. Photo: Gasilov, Leningrad

41 Interior of the Church of the Saviour, Nereditza, 1198. Photo: Gasilov, Leningrad

42 Icon of St Boris and St Gleb, Stroganov school, 17th century. $7\frac{5}{8} \times 9\frac{1}{4}$ (19×23½). Courtesy of George R. Hann Collection, USA

43 Fresco from the Monastery of Mirozhsk, near Pskov, 1156. Photo: L'Œil, Paris

44 Church of St Nicholas, Lipna, Novgorod, 1292. Photo: Gasilov, Leningrad

45 Church of the Saviour, Iliina, Novgorod, 1372. Photo: Gasilov, Leningrad

46 Church of St Theodore Stratelites, Novgorod, 1361–62. Photo: Gasilov, Leningrad

47 Icon of St Nicholas with saints, 12th century Novgorodian work from the Novodevichi Monastery. Now in the Tretyakov Gallery, Moscow. $56 \times 37\frac{1}{4}$ (140×93). Photo: Gasilov, Leningrad

48 Icon of The Saviour of the Fiery Eye, 14th century. Palace of Arms Museum, Moscow. Photo: Gasilov, Leningrad

49 Icon of St George, 12th-century Greek work. Hermitage Museum, Leningrad

50 Icon of St Demetrius of Salonica, school of Pskov, 15th century. Russian Museum, Leningrad. Photo: Gasilov, Leningrad

51 The iconostasis in Polotsk Cathedral, 18th century

52 Icon of the Crucifixion, school of Novgorod, 16th century. Louvre, Paris. Photo: Jacqueline Hyde

53 Icon of St Elias and the Fiery Chariot, school of Novgorod, c. 1500. $21\frac{1}{4} \times 29\frac{7}{8}$ (53·5×75·5). Courtesy of George R. Hann Collection, USA

54 Icon of the Last Judgement, school of Novgorod, 17th century. $58\frac{1}{4} \times 83\frac{1}{4}$ (145·5×208). Courtesy of George R. Hann Collection, USA

55 Biographical icon of St Theodore, 16th century

56 Icon of the Battle between the Men of Novgorod and the Men of Suzdal, school of Novgorod, 15th century. $34\frac{5}{8} \times 26\frac{1}{4}$ (88×66·5). Russian Museum, Leningrad. Photo: Gasilov, Leningrad

57 Detail of a fresco of St George, from the Church of St George, Staraya Ladoga, c. 1185. Photo: Gasilov, Leningrad

58 Detail of a fresco of the Old Testament Trinity, from the Church of the Transfiguration, Novgorod, by Theophanes the Greek, 1378. Photo: Gasilov, Leningrad

59 Fresco of the Head of Abraham, from the Church of the Assumption, Volotovo, c. 1380

60 Carved and pierced walrus ivory writing-desk. Archangel work, 18th century. $11\frac{3}{4} \times 8 \times 4\frac{1}{2}$ (29·5×25×11). Courtesy of the Walters Art Gallery, Baltimore

61 A wooden scoop from Gorbunovo, 2nd millennium B.C. Historical Museum, Moscow. After Alpatov

62 Silver *kovsh* dated to 1635. Courtesy of the Victoria and Albert Museum, London

63 *Kovsh* and scoop of carved wood. Peasant work of 18th-century date. Courtesy of the Victoria and Albert Museum, London. Photo: Eileen Tweedy

64 Wooden church at Kem, 1714. Photo: R. M. M. Crawford

65 Wooden church at Suzdal, 17th century. Photo: Sally Crosse

66 Church of St Nicholas, Panilovo, 1600

67 Church of the Transfiguration, Kizhi, 1714

68 Church of the Trinity, Podporozhie, district of Archangel, 1725–27. After Grabar 1st ed.

69 Country house of wood, 17th century

70 The kremlin and its outer defences at Novgorod. Photo: Courtauld Institute, London

71 The Golden Gate, Vladimir, 1164. Photo: Sally Crosse

72 Cloisonné enamel necklace and pendants, and glass bangles and rings, 11th–12th century. Russian Museum, Leningrad. Photo: Gasilov, Leningrad

73 Carved walrus-bone comb from Northern Russia, 17th century. $2\frac{3}{4} \times 5\frac{1}{4}$ (7×13). Courtesy of the Walters Art Gallery, Baltimore

74 Cloisonné enamel pendant, 12th century. Dumbarton Oaks, USA. Photo: Courtesy of the Dumbarton Oaks Collection—Trustees for Harvard University

75 Bronze aquamanile, 13th century. $7\frac{5}{8} \times 8\frac{1}{2}$ (19·5×21·5). Courtesy of the Walters Art Gallery, Baltimore

76 Cloisonné enamel pendants, 11th–12th century. Diameter 2 (5). Courtesy of the Walters Art Gallery, Baltimore. Photo: James R. Dunlop Inc.

77 The tower of Bogolyubovo Palace, c. 1160. Photo: Sally Crosse

78 Reconstruction of a roof of a medieval house. After Karger

79 The Pogankiny Palaty, Pskov, 17th century

80 Dome of the Church of St Theodore Stratelites, Novgorod, 17th century. After Lukomski

81 Wall of the Kirillo-Bielozersk Monastery, 1635. Photo: Courtauld Institute, London

82 A defence tower at the Kirillo-Bielozersk Monastery. Photo: Courtauld Institute, London

83 The cathedral church of the Vydubetsk Monastery. Photo: Courtauld Institute, London

84 The wooden Palace of Kolomenskoe as it appeared in the 18th century

85 Detail from the Ludogoshchinsk carved wooden cross, 1356. After Alpatov

86 A decorated shuttle, 19th century. Historical Museum, Moscow. After Alpatov

87 Chair and wooden candlestick, from Tikhvin, 17th century. Courtesy of the Victoria and Albert Museum, London

88 Carving in relief of a lion, late 17th–early 18th century. Historical Museum, Moscow. After Alpatov

89 Incised and painted design of a bird, on an 18th-century loom. Historical Museum, Moscow. After Alpatov

276

90 Carved window surround from the Smolensk area, 18th century

91 Carved gingerbread stamp from the district of Vologda, 18th century. Courtesy of the Victoria and Albert Museum, London

92 Cathedral of the Savvino-Storozhevsk Monastery, Zvenigorod, 1405–07. Photo: Sally Crosse

93 The chapel and refectory of the Troitse-Sergieva Lavra, Zagorsk, 17th century. Photo: Sally Crosse

94 Detail of the icon of the Saviour, from the Cathedral of the Annunciation, Moscow, by Theophanes the Greek, 1405. Tretyakov Gallery, Moscow. After Lazarev

95 Detail of the icon of the Saviour, by Andrei Rublev, from the Cathedral of Zvenigorod, early 15th century. $62\frac{1}{4} \times 40\frac{1}{2}$ (158×103). Tretyakov Gallery, Moscow,

96 Illumination from a 15th-century manuscript. Yates Thomson 51. British Museum, London. Courtesy of the Trustees of the British Museum

97 Illumination from a 15th-century manuscript. Yates Thomson 51. British Museum, London. Courtesy of the Trustees of the British Museum

98 Detail from the icon of the Nativity, from the Cathedral of the Annunciation, Moscow, school of Rublev, 1405. Complete panel $24\frac{1}{2} \times 19\frac{1}{4}$ (71×53). Tretyakov Gallery, Moscow. Photo: Gasilov, Leningrad

99 Detail from the icon of the Old Testament Trinity, by Rublev, painted between 1411 and 1422. Complete panel $56\frac{3}{4} \times 45\frac{1}{2}$ (142×114). Tretyakov Gallery, Moscow. Photo: Gasilov, Leningrad

100 Head of Abraham. Fresco in the Cathedral of the Assumption at Vladimir, by Daniel Chorny, *c.* 1408. Photo: Gasilov, Leningrad

101 Icon of Christ in Majesty, by Rublev and Chorny, *c.* 1408. $121\frac{3}{4} \times 94$ (314×220). Tretyakov Gallery, Moscow. Photo: Gasilov, Leningrad

102 Detail from an icon of the Dormition, school of Rublev, 15th century. $57\frac{3}{8} \times 25\frac{1}{4}$ (145×115). Tretyakov Gallery, Moscow

103 The east and north fronts of the Cathedral of the Assumption, Vladimir, 1185–89. Photo: Gasilov, Leningrad

104 The Cathedral of the Assumption, 1475–79, and the Palace of Facets, 1487–91, Moscow. Photo: R. M. M. Crawford

105 Cathedral of the Archangel Michael, Moscow, 1505–09. Photo: C. H. Flurscheim

106 Cathedral of the Annunciation, Moscow, 1482–90. Photo: Alick Barratt

107 The Kremlin at Moscow. Photo: Courtesy of the Trustees of the British Museum, London

108 Church of the Ascension, Kolomenskoe, 1532. After Grabar 1st ed.

109 Cathedral of the Ordination in the Kremlin, Moscow, 1485–86; Church of the Saviour behind the Golden Lattice, 1678, on the left. Photo: Martin Hürlimann

110 Church of St Nicholas, Khamovniki, Moscow, 17th century. Photo: R. M. M. Crawford

111 Church of the Beheading of St John the Baptist, Dyakovo, 1553–54. After Grabar 1st ed.

112 Cathedral of St Basil the Blessed, Moscow, 1555–60. Photo: Alick Barratt

113 Church of the Intercession of the Virgin, Fili, 1693. Photo: Jacques Cantou

114 Church of the Virgin of the Sign, Dubrovitzy, 1690–1704. Photo: Gasilov, Leningrad

115 Fresco of St George and St Demetrius of Salonica in the Cathedral of the Assumption, Moscow, 1508. Photo: Gasilov, Leningrad

116 Interior of the Cathedral of the Assumption, Moscow. Photo: Alick Barratt

117 Icon of the Archangel Gabriel from the Therapont Monastery, by Dionysius. Russian Museum, Leningrad. Photo: Gasilov, Leningrad

118 Illumination from a 16th-century Gospel. Egerton 3. British Museum, London. Courtesy of the Trustees of the British Museum. Photo: Eileen Tweedy

119 Icon of the Last Judgement, Muscovite school, 17th century. Louvre, Paris. Photo: Jacqueline Hyde

120 Icon showing saints and prophets, Stroganov school, late 16th–early 17th century. Courtesy of George R. Hann Collection, USA

121 Portrait icon of Prince Skopin-Shuyski, Moscow school, 17th century. $17\frac{1}{2} \times 13\frac{1}{2}$ ($41 \times 33 \cdot 5$). Tretyakov Gallery, Moscow. After *Peinture de l'Ancienne Russie*

122 Icon of Our Lady of Smolensk, Stroganov school, early 17th century. $10\frac{3}{4} \times 12\frac{1}{4}$ (27×30). Courtesy of George R. Hann Collection, USA

123 The Redeemer Gate, the Kremlin, Moscow. Photo: C. H. Flurscheim

124 The Kremlin at Moscow seen from the south. Photo: Courtesy of the Trustees of the British Museum

125 Map of Moscow's defences. After A. I. Vlasiuk

126 The Novodevichi Monastery, Moscow, founded 1524. Photo: Courtesy of the Trustees of the British Museum

127 Church of the Archangel Gabriel, Moscow, by Zarudnyi, 1705–07. Photo: R. M. M. Crawford

128 The old Printing House, Moscow, 1679 (restored late 19th century). Photo: R. Milner-Gulland

129 The Church of the Ordination in the Donskaya Street, Moscow, 1701. Photo: Jacques Cantou

130 Silver gilt embossed chalice adorned with enamels, 1702. Courtesy of George R. Hann Collection, USA

131 17th-century copper candlesticks

132 Wrought-iron gate of 17th-century Muscovite workmanship. Photo: Courtesy of the Victoria and Albert Museum London

133 Coconut mounted in silver, adorned with scan enamel, 17th century. H. $4\frac{1}{2}$ (11). Courtesy of the Walters Art Gallery, Baltimore

134 Gold censer, 1598. Courtesy of the Kremlin Museum, Moscow

135 Silver censer, 1597. Courtesy of the Historical Museum, Moscow

136 Silver *kovsh*, 1702. Courtesy of Mrs Herbert A. May Collection, Washington DC. Photo: James R. Dunlop Inc.

137 Silver and enamel bowl, 17th century. Courtesy of the Walters Art Gallery, Baltimore. Photo: James R. Dunlop Inc.

138 Silver and niello bowl, 1676–82

139 Embroidered chasuble, 16th century, Muscovite work. Photo: Gasilov, Leningrad

140 Embroidered wedding kerchief, 18th century

141 Embroidered head-dress, Yaroslavl work, 17th century. Photo: Gasilov, Leningrad

142 Gold and silver embroidered bed-hanging, Vladimir work, 17th century

143 Embroidered altar cloth, 17th century. Courtesy of George R. Hann Collection, USA

144 Embroidered portrait shroud of St Sergius of Radonezh, 15th century. Zagorsk Museum. Photo: Gasilov, Leningrad

145 Yaroslavl tile, 18th century

146 Pottery jug from Rostov, 17th century

147 The church in the Fortress of St Peter and St Paul, St Petersburg, by Tressini, 1714–25. Photo: Gasilov, Leningrad

148 The Kunstkamera, St Petersburg, by Mattarnovi, 1718–25. Photo: Gasilov, Leningrad

149 The Summer Gardens. A 19th-century print by Sadovnikov

150 The Hermitage Theatre, St Petersburg, water-colour by Alexander Benois, c. 1904. Photo: Nicholas Talbot Rice

151 The Winter Palace, St Petersburg, begun by Rastrelli in 1755. Photo: Alick Barratt

152 Cathedral of the Smolny Convent, St Petersburg, by Rastrelli, 1748–64. Photo: Gasilov, Leningrad

153 The Moika canal front of the Stroganov Palace, St Petersburg, by Rastrelli, 1752–54. Photo: G. C. Griffith

154 Cathedral of St Andrew, Kiev, by Rastrelli, 1747. Photo: Sally Crosse

155 Entrance to New Holland, St Petersburg, by Vallin de la Mothe, 18th century. After Grabar 1st ed.

156 Bridge at Tsaritsyno Palace by V. I. Bazhenov, late 18th century. Photo: Royal Institute of British Architects

157 Main entrance to the Admiralty, St Petersburg, by Zakharov, 1806–23. Photo: Martin Hürlimann

158 The Stock Exchange, St Petersburg, by Thomas de Thomon. Photo: Alick Barratt

159 The Palace Square and General Staff Headquarters, St Petersburg, by Rossi

160 Theatre Street, St Petersburg, by Rossi. After Grabar 1st ed.

161 The main cascade, Peterhof. Photo: Alick Barratt

162 The Cameron Gallery at Tsarskoe Selo, by Cameron, 1783–85. Photo: C. H. Cruft

163 The Palace of Oranienbaum, by Rinaldi, 18th-century engraving. Courtesy of the Trustees of the British Museum, London

164 The Toboggan Hill at Oranienbaum, by Rinaldi. Photo: Gasilov, Leningrad

165 The Catherine Palace at Tsarskoe Selo, by Rastrelli, 1749–56. Photo: Gasilov, Leningrad

166 The Palace of Pavlovsk, by Cameron, 1781–96. Photo: C. H. Cruft

167 The Green Dining Room at the Catherine Palace, Tsarskoe Selo, by Cameron

168 The Cabinet of Mirrors at the Catherine Palace, Tsarskoe Selo, by Cameron

169 Late-18th-century table in gilt wood, carved and fitted with malachite top. Ickworth House

170 Early-19th-century urn in malachite. Diameter 27 (68·5). Private collection. Photo: Eileen Tweedy

171 Sculpture of St George, by Ermolin, c. 1480. Tretyakov Gallery, Moscow. Photo: R. Milner-Gulland

172 Bronze bust of Peter the Great, by Rastrelli the elder, 1724. The Hermitage, Leningrad. Photo: Gasilov, Leningrad

173 Memorial to Princess Gagarina, by Martos, in the Lazarus cemetery, Leningrad. Photo: Gasilov, Leningrad

174 Monument to General Suvorov, by Kozlovski, Leningrad. Photo: Gasilov, Leningrad

175 Marble bust of Count A. G. Orlovski, by Fedot Shubin, 1771. Russian Museum, Leningrad. Photo: Gasilov, Leningrad

176 Bronze equestrian group on the Anichkov Bridge, Leningrad, by Baron Klodt, 1839. Photo: R. Milner-Gulland

177 Enamel plaques of two archangels, c. 1680–1700. Courtesy of the Walters Art Gallery, Baltimore. Photo: James R. Dunlop Inc.

178 Chair in cut steel. Tula Foundry, 18th century. Courtesy of the Victoria and Albert Museum, London. Photo: John R. Freeman & Co.

179 Mantelpiece, fender, fire-irons, and ornaments in Tula cut steel, 18th century. Perfume burner: H. 18½, Diameter 6⅝ (46×16). Two urns: H. 14, Diameter 4 18/16 (35×11). Courtesy of the Victoria and Albert Museum, London. Photo: John R. Freeman & Co.

180 Coffee set in white enamel on copper, 18th century. Tray: 8×5½ (20×14). Cups: H. 1½, Diameter 2 (3·5×5). Tamara Talbot Rice Collection. Photo: Eileen Tweedy

181 Gold chalice, St Petersburg, 1791. H. 13 (33). Photo: Courtesy of C. & H. Wartski (Llandudno) Limited

182 *Bonbonnière*, Ador, St Petersburg. Louvre, Paris. Photo: Archives photographiques, Paris

183 Snuff-box with portrait in enamel, St Petersburg, 1773. 1¼×3¼ (3×8). Courtesy of Mrs Herbert A. May Collection, Washington DC. Photo: James R. Dunlop Inc.

184 Gilt and engraved glass, 18th century. Courtesy of Mrs Herbert A. May Collection, Washington DC. Photo: James R. Dunlop Inc.

185 Miniature of Catherine the Great in gold frame. The frame bears the St Petersburg hallmark and the date 1784. Diameter 3¼ (8). Courtesy of Mrs Herbert A. May Collection, Washington DC. Photo: James R. Dunlop Inc.

186 Watch and *chatelaine* bearing Catherine II's monogram. H. 6, Diameter of watch, 1⅝ (15×3). Courtesy of Mrs Herbert A. May Collection, Washington DC. Photo: James R. Dunlop Inc.

187 Gold snuff-box commemorating the *coup d'état* of 1764, by Ador. Courtesy of the Smithsonian Institute, Washington DC

188 Imperial Porcelain Factory vase with ormolu mounts and handles, 18th century. H. 23½ (59). Courtesy of Mrs Herbert A. May Collection, Washington DC. Photo: James R. Dunlop Inc.

189 Girandole, 18th century. H. 28½ (71). Courtesy of Mrs Herbert A. May Collection, Washington DC. Photo: James R. Dunlop Inc.

190 Imperial Porcelain Factory plate marked with the cypher of Elizabeth I. Diameter 12¼ (30). Courtesy of Mrs Herbert A. May Collection, Washington DC. Photo: James R. Dunlop Inc.

191 Pair of vases from the Baktiny Factory, early 19th century. Courtesy of Mrs Herbert A. May Collection, Washington DC. Photo: James R. Dunlop Inc.

192 Imperial Porcelain Factory plate with the initials of Paul I and his wife. Diameter 14 (35). Courtesy of Mrs Herbert A. May Collection, Washington DC. Photo: James R. Dunlop Inc.

193 Carved wooden textile stamp, *c.* 1800. Smolensk Museum. After Alpatov

194 Bessarabian *kilim*, 19th century. 147× 56 (373×142). Photo: Courtesy of the House of Perez, London

195 Lustre tea service, Imperial Porcelain Factory, *c.* 1820. Courtesy of Mrs Herbert A. May Collection, Washington DC. Photo: James R. Dunlop Inc.

196 Imperial Porcelain Factory plate bearing the cypher of Nicholas I. Diameter 10 (24½). Courtesy of Mrs Herbert A. May Collection, Washington DC. Photo: James R. Dunlop Inc.

197 Tea service, by Gardner, *c.* 1820. Courtesy of Mrs Herbert A. May Collection, Washington DC. Photo: James R. Dunlop Inc.

198 19th-century brocade. Courtesy of the Victoria and Albert Museum, London. Photo: Eileen Tweedy

199 Portrait of Yakov Turgenev, by Adolski, *c.* 1695. Oil on canvas. Russian Museum, Leningrad. After Alpatov

200 Portrait of Princess Dashkova, by Levitski, 1784. Oil on canvas, 23½ × 19½ (59 × 49). Courtesy of Mrs Herbert A. May Collection, Washington DC. Photo: James R. Dunlcp Inc.

201 Portrait of a Peasant girl, by Argunov, 1784. Oil on canvas. Photo: Gasilov, Leningrad

202 Portrait of the Ataman Krasnoshchekhov, by Antropov, 1761. Oil on canvas, 24 × 17½ (61 × 42·5). Russian Museum, Leningrad. Photo: Gasilov, Leningrad

203 Portrait of Mrs Surovtseva, by Rokotov, 1780. Oil on canvas, 27 × 20¾ (67·5 × 52). Photo: Gasilov, Leningrad

204 Portrait of Mrs Skobeeva, by Borovikovski. Oil on canvas, 26 × 21½ (65·5 × 54). Russian Museum, Leningrad. Photo: Gasilov, Leningrad

205 *Dancing Bacchante*, by Bazhenov after Poussin, 1784. Drawing. Photo: Royal Institute of British Architects

206 *The Rider*, by Brüllov, 1832. Oil on canvas. Tretyakov Gallery, Moscow. After Grabar 1st ed.

207 Self-portrait, by Kiprenski. Oil on canvas. Russian Museum, Leningrad

208 Portrait of K. G. Ravich, by V. A. Tropinin, 1825. Oil on canvas. Russian Museum, Leningrad

209 A *lubok*, illustrating Kryllov's fable *The Industrious Bear*. Tamara Talbot Rice Collection

210 Study for an Imbecile, by Surikov, 1887. Oil on canvas, 26¾ × 21¾ (66·5 × 54·5)

211 *View of St Petersburg*, by Alekseev, 1799. Oil on canvas. Photo: Gasilov, Leningrad

212 *Christ before the People*, by A. A. Ivanov, 1833–55. Oil on canvas. Russian Museum, Leningrad. Photo: Gasilov, Leningrad

213 *Peasant children in a Field*, by Venetsianov, 1820. Oil on canvas

214 *A Poor Aristocrat's Breakfast*, by Fedotov. Oil on canvas

215 *A Monastic Refectory*, by Perov, 1865–75. Oil on canvas, 33½ × 50½ (84 × 126). Russian Museum, Leningrad. Photo: Gasilov, Leningrad

216 Portrait of a Miller, by Kramskoi. Oil on canvas. Photo: Gasilov, Leningrad

217 *Leo Tolstoy at work*, portrait by Repin. Water-colour. Russian Museum, Leningrad. Photo: Gasilov, Leningrad

218 *They did not expect him*, by Repin, 1884. Oil on canvas, 41¾ × 65¾ (106·5 × 167·5). Tretyakov Gallery, Moscow. Photo: Camilla Gray

219 *Girls*, by Malyavin. A detail. Oil on canvas. Russian Museum, Leningrad. Photo: Gasilov, Leningrad

220 *The Bogatyr*, by Vrubel, 1898. A decorative panel. Russian Museum, Leningrad. Photo: Gasilov, Leningrad

221 *Girls with Peaches*, a portrait, by Serov, 1887. Oil on canvas. Photo: Gasilov, Leningrad

222 Portrait of Nicholas II, by Serov, 1900. Oil on canvas

223 Abramtzevo House, near Moscow. Photo: R. M. M. Crawford

224 *A Warrior at the Crossroads*, by V. Vasnetsov, 1882. Oil on canvas, 66¾ × 119½ (167 × 299). Russian Museum, Leningrad. Photo: Gasilov, Leningrad

225 *A sketch*, by Stelletski. After *Zhar Ptitza*

226 *October 1917*, by Favorski. Engraving. Courtesy of Eric Estorick

227 Costume sketch, by Korovin, 1908. Pastel, 14⅝ × 11 (37 × 28). Tamara Talbot Rice Collection

228 Backcloth for the opera *The Nightingale*, by Golovin. Photo: Eileen Tweedy. After *Zhar Ptitza*, no. 10

229 Costume design for *The Sleeping Princess*, by Léon Bakst. Fitzwilliam Museum, Cambridge. Photo: Thames and Hudson archive

230 Curtain for *Coq d'Or*, by Alexander Benois, 1927

231 *A Sunny Spring Day*, by Yuon, 1904. Oil on canvas. Russian Museum, Leningrad. Photo: Gasilov, Leningrad

232 *Interior*, by M. Dobuzhinski, *c.* 1927. Oil on canvas. V. Dobuzhinski Collection

233 *1918 in Petrograd*, by Petrov-Vodkin, 1920. Oil on canvas, 28¼ × 36½ (73 × 92). Tretyakov Gallery, Moscow. Photo: Camilla Gray

234 *The Reservoir*, by Borissov-Mussatov, 1902. Tempera on paper. Tretyakov Gallery, Moscow. Photo: Camilla Gray

235 *Russian Soldiers*, by Marc Chagall, 1917. Tempera, 15½ × 12½ (39 × 30). Courtesy of Eric Estorick

236 *Monk with Cat*, by Natalia Goncharova, 1910. Oil on canvas, 39½ × 36¼ (100 × 92). National Gallery of Modern Art, Edinburgh. Courtesy of the Trustees of the National Galleries of Scotland. Photo: Tom Scott

237 *Soldier in a Wood*, by Larionov, 1908–09. Oil on canvas, 33¼ × 36½ (85 × 93). National Gallery of Modern Art, Edinburgh. Courtesy of the Trustees of the National Galleries of Scotland. Photo: Tom Scott

238 *Man in a Cellar*, by B. Grigoriev. Oil on canvas. After *Zhar Ptitza*, no. 11

239 *Cityscape*, by A Exter, *c.* 1916. Oil on canvas. Photo: Camilla Gray

240 Icon of the Archangel Michael, school of Novgorod, 16th century. 15¾ × 33 (39 × 82·5). Courtesy of George R. Hann Collection, USA

241 *An Evangelist*, by Natalia Goncharova, 1910. Oil on canvas, 80½ × 23 (204 × 58). Photo: Thames and Hudson archive

242 *Composition from a Nude*, by Vladimir Tatlin, 1913. Oil on canvas, 56¼ × 42½ (143 × 103). Tretyakov Gallery, Moscow. Photo: Camilla Gray

243 Portrait of Tatlin, by Mikhail Larionov, 1913–14. Oil on canvas, 35½ × 28¼ (90 × 72). Michel Seuphor Collection, Paris. Photo: Camilla Gray

244 *Yellow Quadrilateral on White*, by Kasimir Malevich, 1916–17. Oil on canvas, 41¾ × 23¾ (106 × 70·5). Stedelijk Museum, Amsterdam. Photo: Thames and Hudson archive

245 *Composition No.* 2, by Kandinski, 1910. Oil on canvas, 78¾ × 108¼ (200 × 275). Formerly Baron von Gamp Collection, Berlin. Photo: Thames and Hudson archive

246 Tatlin working on the Monument of the Third International, by El Lissitski. Photo: Courtesy of Eric Estorick

247 Stage set for the ballet *La Chatte*, by Pevsner and Gabo, 1927

248 *Skulpturmalerei*, by Archipenko, 1915. 18 × 17½ (45 × 44). Courtesy of Eric Estorick

249 *Construction 1922*, by Naum Gabo. Courtesy of Naum Gabo

250 *Women Bathing*, by Shukhaev. Oil on canvas. After *Zhar Ptitza*, no. 6

251 *Russian Toys*, by Sudeikin. Oil on canvas. After *Zhar Ptitza*, nos. 4–5

282

Index

All numbers refer to text pages; those in italic indicate illustrations